"Through detailed examples and exercises, we learn how to calm the mind and optimize opportunities to connect with others. Underlying this beautifully written narrative is the view that through positive experience of oneself and others, our brains rewire to promote benevolence, generosity, gratitude, and compassion."

—Stephen Porges, Ph.D., distinguished university scientist, Kinsey Institute, Indiana University; professor of psychiatry, University of North Carolina

"Written with dignity and grace, this book offers a wealth of insights and practical skills for staying strong in the face of adversity. It is a guide to living with integrity, illustrated with disarmingly candid personal observations and supported by scientific research."

—Christopher Germer, Ph.D., lecturer, Harvard Medical School; author of The Mindful Path to Self-Compassion

"In the chaos of uncertainty and adversity, one calm person in the room can make all the difference, and Rick Hanson shows us how to be that person. Resilient offers highly accessible methods to overcome the brain's negativity bias and find our way to buoyancy rather than burn out. This book is an immeasurable resource and gift for well-being."

—Frank Ostaseski, author of The Five Invitations: Discovering What Death Can Teach Us About Living Fully

"This clear, comprehensive, and kind guide is a science-backed compendium of simple practices and insightful wisdom for the challenging world we face each day."

—Daniel J. Siegel, M.D., author of Mind: A Journey to the Heart of Being Human and Aware: The Science and Practice of Presence

"Resilient is a wise and compassionate book. It's a beautiful hands-on guide to foster balance, happiness, and health. In reading these pages, you can literally feel Rick and Forrest's sincere and kind voices guiding us to grow wiser and more grounded. This is truly a special and rare offering. Wow!"

—Bob Stahl, Ph.D., coauthor of A Mindfulness-Based Stress Reduction Workbook; Living with Your Heart Wide Open; Calming the Rush of Panic; A Mindfulness-Based Stress Reduction Workbook for Anxiety; and MBSR Everyday

"Rooted in brain science and positive psychology, this book is a treasure trove of best practices for maintaining sustainable, undentable joy. It is precisely what we have come to expect from Rick Hanson: a book that is practical, empirical, readable, and deeply wise."

—Robert A. Emmons, Ph.D., editor in chief, The Journal of Positive Psychology; author of The Little Book of Gratitude and Gratitude Works!

"Dr. Hanson covers a large amount of helpful information in easy-to-read language containing much richness and wisdom. There are specific examples of how to grow resources, and this book is well worth the read."

—Sandra Prince-Embury, Ph.D., The Resiliency Institute of Allenhurst; developer of widely used scales measuring resilience; and coeditor of Resilience in Children, Adolescents, and Adults: Translating Research into Practice

"Rick Hanson is a perfect guide for these times. In Resilient, he is both wise and scientific, practical and expansive. He names the often unconscious tilt toward negativity that so many of us have and a way to rewire our brains—and therefore, our entire orientation to being alive. His words are so reassuring, so useful, so easy to implement even when we think it and we are hopeless. If we are to make it through these challenging times, it will be by being resilient—and have Resilient by our sides."

—Geneen Roth, author of the #1 New York Times bestseller Women Food and God and This Messy Magnificent Life

"With humor, warmth, honesty, and a gift for making complicated ideas come alive, Dr. Hanson weaves together insights from neurobiology, modern psychology, and ancient wisdom traditions to provide easy-to-use tools to care for both our heads and our hearts. This is an essential resource not only to survive but to grow during difficult times."

—Ronald D. Siegel, Psy.D., assistant professor of psychology, Harvard Medical School; author of The Mindfulness Solution: Everyday Practices for Everyday Problems

"Tremendously practical neuroscience. Resilient is wise and helpful: skill building for the brain, medicine for the heart, and guidance for living a beautiful and enjoyable life."

—Jack Kornfield, Ph.D., author of A Path with Heart

"Rick Hanson has transformed many lives with his tools for creating positive plasticity in the brain. Resilient takes the science to a new level. You will learn about inner strengths you didn't know you had, and how to use them to live your best life, every day."

—Elissa Epel, Ph.D., professor, University of California, San Francisco; coauthor of The Telomere Effect: A Revolutionary Approach to Living Younger, Healthier, Longer

"Today there is an epidemic of stress, anxiety, and depression. The key to not only surviving but thriving is the development of resilience. Marshaling years of experience combined with the latest science, Rick Hanson gives us a guide for developing resilient well-being. Thoughtful, profound, and practical."

—James R. Doty, M.D., founder and director of the Center for Compassion and Altruism Research and Education at Stanford University; author of Into the Magic Shop: A Neurosurgeon's Quest to Discover the Mysteries of the Brain and the Secrets of the Heart

"We live in a world of rapid change, and sometimes it seems like each day brings a new crisis or disaster. These days, we all need to grow tools that help us stay focused, courageous, and wise in the face of real and imaginary danger. Rick Hanson shows us how."

—Christine Carter, Ph.D., author of Raising Happiness and The Sweet Spot

"The clarity of Dr. Hanson's thoughts and writing emerge from a deep and profound understanding of how we can learn to be more compassionate, calm, and resilient. Everyone who reads this book will find something valuable and useful."

—Robert D. Truog, M.D., Frances Glessner Lee Professor of Medical Ethics, Anaesthesia, and Pediatrics, Harvard Medical School

"Rick Hanson guides us in how to cultivate well-being through learning to hold in mind what is helpful, enjoyable, and promotes flourishing. Here is a book of immense wisdom and practicality. Written in a clear, inviting, and friendly style, it can help all of us to cultivate a mind that is more able to induce happiness for ourselves and others."

—Paul Gilbert. Ph.D., O.B.E., founder of Compassion Focused Therapy; author of The Compassionate Mind and Living Like Crazy

"Rick Hanson weaves together theory and direct experience, sharing honest examples from his own life and simple, practical exercises that prompt the reader into liberating explorations of their own."

—Sharon Salzberg, author of Real Happiness and Real Love

"Rick Hanson is not only wise and compassionate, he is also brilliant at systematizing complex material into bite-sized, easy-to-understand pieces."

—Daniel Ellenberg, Ph.D., founder of Rewire Leadership Institute

"In the jungle of books on mindfulness and neuroscience, Rick Hanson hacks a comprehensive and enlightening path through, while giving insight on how to understand your wild and wooly mind. And if that wasn't enough, he gives us tools to achieve peace and happiness. What more could you ask for?"

—Ruby Wax, O.B.E., author of Sane New World; A Mindfulness Guide for the Frazzled; and How to Be Human: The Manual

"Resilient is a kind and supportive book that provides welcome wisdom for our increasingly chaotic world."

—Michael D. Yapko, Ph.D., author of Mindfulness and Hypnosis and Depression Is Contagious

"The authors both explore our capacities for enduring well-being and give us the practical tools to transform our lives."

—Elisha Goldstein, Ph.D., founder of A Course in Mindful Living

"Clear, accessible, and wise, this book sums up how to be a better friend to yourself rather than your own worst critic. It can be life-changing for you and for your family."

—Mark Williams, Ph.D., coauthor of The Mindful Way through Depression

"Grounded in the latest neuroscience of happiness, Resilient is brimming with insight, engaging practices, and clarity that is so needed in these stressful times. Read it, and you will find the many riches of the resilient mind."

—Dacher Keltner, Ph.D., professor of psychology, UC Berkeley; author of Born to Be Good and The Power Paradox

Resilient

ALSO BY RICK HANSON

Hardwiring Happiness

Just One Thing

Buddha's Brain

Mother Nurture

Resilient

How to Grow an Unshakable Core of Calm, Strength, and Happiness

Rick Hanson, Ph.D.

With Forrest Hanson

 HARMONY
BOOKS · NEW YORK

Published in the United States by Harmony Books, an imprint of the Crown Publishing Group, a division of Penguin Random House LLC, New York. harmonybooks.com

Harmony Books is a registered trademark, and the Circle colophon is a trademark of Penguin Random House LLC.

Library of Congress Cataloging-in-Publication data is available upon request.

ISBN 978-0-451-49884-7
Ebook ISBN 978-0-451-49885-4

Printed in the United States of America

Jacket design by Sarah Horgan
Jacket image: Park Ji Sun/Shutterstock

10 9 8 7 6 5 4 3 2 1

First Edition

To our parents

CONTENTS

ACKNOWLEDGMENTS

This book draws on a large scholarly literature about well-being, resilience, neuroplasticity, and related topics. While there are too many sources to name all of them individually, we would like to offer our respectful gratitude to Richard Davidson, Jim Doty, Angela Duckworth, Carol Dweck, Daniel Ellenberg, Barbara Fredrickson, Christopher Germer, Paul Gilbert, Timothea Goddard, Elisha Goldstein, Linda Graham, Jon Kabat-Zinn, Todd Kashdan, Dachar Keltner, Suniya Luthar, Sonya Lyubomirsky, Ann Masten, Kristin Neff, Stephen Porges, Sandra Prince-Embury, Martin Seligman, Michelle Shiota, Dan Siegel, and Emiliana Simon-Thomas.

We have also drawn on the wisdom and support of key teachers, including Tara Brach, Gil Fronsdal, Jack Kornfield, Ajahn Passano, and Sharon Salzberg.

We are indebted to our colleagues who helped create the Foundations of Well-Being online program, including Jenna Chandler, Karey Gauthier, Laurel Hanson, Michelle Keane, Marion Reynolds, Andrew Schuman, Carisa Speth, Matt States, and most of all Stephanie and David Veillon. We're grateful to readers who gave us useful feedback on drafts of this book and related writings, including Penny Fenner, Elizabeth Ferreira, Emma Hutton-Thamm, Lily O'Brien, Michael Taft, and our superbly capable and kind agent, Amy Rennert. Our editor at Harmony Books, Donna Loffredo, has been an absolute pleasure and a gift to work with, and she and her colleagues have been instrumental in bringing this book into being.

Special love and thanks to Jan and Laurel Hanson.

Resilient

INTRODUCTION

I started out in the human potential movement in the 1970s and am now a clinical psychologist, with a deep interest in neuroscience and mindfulness training along the way. This book summarizes what I've learned about helping people heal from the past, cope with the present, and build a better future.

There's a fundamental idea in psychology and medicine that the path your life takes depends on just three causes: how you manage your challenges, protect your vulnerabilities, and increase your resources. These causes are located in three places: your world, your body, and your mind. When you combine the causes and the places, there are nine ways to make your life better.

All of these are important, but growing resources in the mind has a unique power. It offers the greatest opportunity, since you usually have more influence over your mind than over your body or world. It also offers the greatest impact, since you take your mind with you wherever you go. You can't always count on the world, other people, or even your own body. But you *can* count on durable inner strengths hardwired into your nervous system—and this book is about growing them.

Mental resources like determination, self-worth, and kindness are what make us *resilient*: able to cope with adversity and push through challenges in the pursuit of opportunities. While resilience helps us recover from loss and trauma, it offers much more than that. True resilience fosters well-being, an underlying sense of happiness, love, and peace. Remarkably, as you internalize experiences of well-being, that builds inner strengths which in turn make you more resilient. Well-being and resilience promote each other in an upward spiral.

The key is knowing how to turn passing experiences into lasting inner resources built into your brain. This is *positive neuroplasticity*, and I'll show you how to use it to grow resilient well-being.

CHANGING THE BRAIN

Changing your mind for the better means changing your brain for the better. The brain is continually remodeling itself as you learn from your experiences. When you repeatedly stimulate a "circuit" in your brain, you strengthen it. You learn to be calmer or more compassionate the same way you learn anything else: through repeated practice.

We develop mental resources in two stages. First, we need to experience what we want to grow, such as feeling grateful, loved, or confident. Second—critically important—we must convert that passing experience into a lasting change in the nervous system. Otherwise there is no healing, no growth, no learning. Simply having useful, enjoyable experiences is not enough. This is the central weakness in much positive psychology, human resources training, coaching, and psychotherapy. Most of the beneficial experiences that people have are wasted on their brains. But with just a little effort, you can help them leave enduring traces behind, and I'll show you many effective ways to do this—most of them in the flow of everyday life.

It might sound complicated, but it's actually simple and intuitive. The brain operates so so—with neurons routinely firing five to fifty times a second—that you can grow resilience and well-being many times a day, taking a minute or less each time. It's not a quick fix. You must work the brain the same way you would work a muscle to change it for good: lots of little efforts add up over time. You can trust the results because you'll have earned them.

WALKING THE PATH

It's a cliché but still true: life is a journey. Down that long road, we need supplies and tools, and I've put the best ones I know in these pages. We'll explore how to grow and use these inner strengths to meet your own needs. And then you'll have even more to offer for the needs of other people.

We all have needs. If they're not met, it's natural to feel stressed, worried, frustrated, and hurt, and to experience less well-being. As you become more resilient, you're more able to meet your needs in the face of life's challenges, and greater well-being is the result.

Every human being has three basic needs—*safety*, *satisfaction*, and *connection*—that are grounded in our ancient evolutionary history. While our circumstances have changed enormously over the last two hundred thousand years, our brains have remained largely the same. The neural machinery that enabled our ancestors to satisfy their need for safety by finding shelter, for satisfaction by getting food, and for connection by bonding with others is alive in our brains today.

We meet our needs in four major ways: by *recognizing* what's true, *resourcing* ourselves, *regulating* thoughts, feelings, and actions, and *relating* skillfully to others and the wider world. When we apply these four ways to meet our needs to the three needs we all have, that suggests twelve primary inner strengths, which are the chapters of this book:

	RECOGNIZING	RESOURCING	REGULATING	RELATING
Safety	Compassion	Grit	Calm	Courage
Satisfaction	Mindfulness	Gratitude	Motivation	Aspiration
Connection	Learning	Confidence	Intimacy	Generosity

You can develop these psychological resources in a step-by-step way, like walking a path. It begins with compassion—initially for yourself, since recognizing your own deep needs and feeling moved to do something about them is the necessary first step. The path concludes with generosity, because growing the good inside yourself gives you more and more to offer to others.

As you grow these strengths and become more resilient, you will feel less anxiety and irritation, less disappointment and frustration, and less loneliness, hurt, and resentment. And when the waves of life come at you, you'll meet them with more *peace, contentment,* and *love* in the core of your being.

HOW TO USE THIS BOOK

We'll be exploring the practical *how* of experiencing, growing, and using key mental resources for resilient well-being. You'll see useful ideas about the brain, experiential practices, tools for building specific strengths, suggestions for everyday life, and personal examples. Different things work for different people, and I want to give you a lot of options. Find what's best for you.

You can use this book in a variety of ways. You could explore a new chapter each month for a year of personal growth. Or pick a need that's particularly important to you, such as safety, and focus on the chapters related to it. The twelve strengths support each other like the nodes of a network that are connected together. Some strengths will seem especially relevant to you, and it is fine to jump around and find what speaks to you the most. Chapter 2, "Mindfulness," and Chapter 3, "Learning," cover foundational principles and techniques that underpin the rest of the material. When you come to an experiential practice, you can read it slowly while you do it, or you could read it aloud and record it and then listen to the recording as a kind of guided meditation for yourself.

This book is not psychotherapy or a treatment for any condition. Nonetheless, I've tried to get to the heart of the matter, and that can stir things up. Be kind to yourself, especially when engaging the experiential practices. Always adapt my approach to your own needs.

Useful information can be found in many places, including in science, clinical psychology, and the contemplative traditions. Because we're covering a lot of ground, I've simplified the neurological explanations, and not listed specific therapies and trainings or attempted to summarize the large body of academic literature about resilience, well-being, and related topics. Please see the additional resources section in the back of the book for further exploration, as well as the slide sets, research papers, and other freely offered material at www.RickHanson.net. In terms of contemplative practice, the tradition I know best is Buddhism, and I'll offer some ideas and methods from it. This book is based on my online experiential program, the Foundations of Well-Being (www.thefoundationsofwell-being.com), but does not follow its structure exactly.

For simplicity, the authorial voice here is the "I" of Rick Hanson. Still, Forrest's thoughts and words are on every page. He's contributed tremendous clarity and insight to this material, and it's been an honor and a delight to write this book with my son. Truly, this is a joint effort. Together, we've tried to offer a useful, get-right-to-it, heartfelt book.

We hope you enjoy it.

PART ONE

RECOGNIZING

CHAPTER 1

COMPASSION

*If I am not for myself, then who will be
for me? If not now, when?*

—Rabbi Hillel

One of the most important experiences of my life happened when I was six years old. My family lived in Illinois, on the edge of cornfields. I remember standing outside early one evening, looking down at the rainwater in the ruts left by tractors, and then looking back at our house. I felt wistful and sad about the anger inside it. There were lights twinkling in the distant hills, the homes of other, perhaps happier families.

As an adult today, I can see that my parents were loving, decent people dealing with their own stresses, and that my childhood was fortunate in many ways. My dad had a tough job and my mom had her hands full with my sister and me. I don't remember what happened in our home that night. It could have been an ordinary argument. But as if it were yesterday, I remember feeling a caring toward myself. I felt bad, those feelings mattered, and I wanted to help myself feel better. Many years later, I learned that this was *compassion*—the recognition of pain with the desire to relieve it—which can be given to oneself much as it can be given to others.

I clearly recall knowing that it would be up to me to get through the time ahead, and to find those lights and those people and that greater happiness. I loved my parents and wasn't against anyone. But I was for myself. I was determined—as a child can be, and an adult as well—to have as good a life as I could.

My own path of well-being began with compassion, as it does for most people. Compassion for yourself is fundamental, since if you don't care how you feel and want to *do* something about it, it's hard to make an effort to become happier and more resilient. Compassion is both soft and muscular. For example, studies show that when people feel compassion, motor planning areas in the brain begin preparing for action.

Compassion is a psychological resource, an *inner strength*. In this chapter, we'll explore how to grow compassion and use it for yourself, and in later chapters, we'll see how to bring compassion to others.

BE FOR YOURSELF

When we treat others with respect and caring, the best in them usually comes out. Much the same would happen if we could treat ourselves the same way.

Yet most of us are a better friend to others than we are to ourselves. We care about their pain, see positive qualities in them, and treat them fairly and kindly. But what kind of friend are you to yourself? Many people are tough on themselves, critical, second-guessing and self-doubting, tearing down rather than building up.

Imagine treating yourself like you would a friend. You'd be encouraging, warm, and sympathetic, and you'd help yourself heal and grow. Think about what a typical day would be like if you were on your own side. What would it feel like to appreciate your good intentions and good heart, and be less self-critical?

Why It's Good to Be Good to Yourself

It helps to understand the reasons it's both fair and important to be on your own side. Otherwise, beliefs like these can take over: "It's selfish to think about what you want." "You don't deserve love." "Deep down you're bad." "You'll fail if you dream bigger dreams."

First, there's the general principle that we should treat people with decency and compassion. Well, "people" includes the person who wears your name tag. The Golden Rule is a two-way street: we should do unto ourselves as we do unto others.

Second, the more influence we have over someone, the more responsibility we have to treat them well. For example, surgeons have great power over their patients, so they have a great duty to be careful when they operate on them. Who's the one person you can affect the most? It's *yourself*, both you in this moment and your future self: the person you will be in the next minute, week, or year. If you think of yourself as someone to whom you have a duty of care and kindness, what might change in how you talk to yourself, and in how you go about your day?

Third, being good to yourself is good for others. When people increase their own well-being, they usually become more patient, cooperative, and caring in their relationships. Think about how it would benefit others if you felt less stressed, worried, or irritated, and more peaceful, contented, and loving.

You can take practical steps to help yourself really believe that it's good to treat yourself with respect and compassion. You could write down simple statements—such as "I am on my own side" or "I'm taking a stand for myself" or "I matter, too"—and read them aloud to yourself or put them somewhere you'll see each day. You could imagine telling someone why you are going to take better care of your own needs. Or imagine a friend, a mentor, or even your fairy godmother telling you to be on your own side—and let them talk you into it!

The Feeling of Caring for Yourself

When I left home for UCLA in 1969, I was hyper-rational and stuck in my head. This was a way to avoid feeling sad, hurt, and worried, but then I didn't feel much of anything at all. I had to get in touch with myself in order to heal and grow. California in the 1970s was at the center of the human potential movement, and I dove in even though it seemed kind of freaky. (Primal screaming! Encounter groups! Bare your soul on demand!) I gradually learned to tune into my emotions and body sensations in general. In particular, I started paying attention to what it felt like to get on my own side, and to have warmth and support toward myself instead of coldness and criticism. It felt good to do this, so I kept doing it. Each time I focused on these positive experiences was like working a muscle and strengthening it, again and again. With repetition, kindness and encouragement for myself gradually sank in and became a natural way of being.

Many years later as a psychologist, I learned how my intuitive efforts had worked. Focusing on and staying with any experience of a psychological resource—such as the sense of being for yourself—is a powerful way to reinforce it in your brain. Then you take that inner strength with you wherever you go.

In the chapters on Mindfulness and Learning, I'll explain in detail how to turn your thoughts and feelings into lasting strengths inside: the basis of true resilience. The essence is simple: first, experience what you want to develop in yourself—such as compassion or gratitude—and second, focus on it and keep it going to increase its consolidation in your nervous system.

This is the fundamental process of positive brain change. To get a sense of it, try the practice in the box. It takes only a minute or two, or you can slow it down for a deeper effect. Like anything I suggest, adapt it to your own needs. Additionally, in the flow of everyday life, notice when you have an attitude or feeling of caring for yourself, and then stay with the experience for a few extra moments, feeling it in your body, sinking into it as it sinks into you.

BEING FOR YOURSELF

Bring to mind a time when you were on somebody's side: perhaps a child you were protecting, a friend you were encouraging, or an aging parent with health issues. Recall what this felt like in your body—in the set of your shoulders, in the expression on your face. Recall some of your thoughts and feelings—perhaps caring, determination, even a fierce intensity.

Then, knowing what it's like to be on someone's side, apply this attitude to yourself. Get a sense of being an ally to yourself—someone who will look out for you, help you, protect you. Recognize that you have rights and needs that matter.

It's normal if other reactions come up, such as feeling unworthy. Just notice and disengage from them, and then come back to the sense of wishing yourself well. Focus on this experience, and stay with it for a couple breaths or longer.

Bring to mind times when you were really on your own side. Perhaps you were encouraging yourself during a tough period at work or speaking up to someone who hurt you. Get a sense of what that was like, emotionally and in your body. Remember some of the thoughts you had, such as "It's only fair for others to help, too." Stay with this experience and let it fill your mind.

Know what it's like to be committed to your own well-being. Let the feelings, thoughts, and intentions of being a true friend to yourself sink in, becoming a part of you.

BRING COMPASSION TO YOUR PAIN

Compassion is a warmhearted sensitivity to suffering—from subtle mental or physical discomfort to agonizing pain—along with the desire to help if you can. Giving compassion lowers stress and calms your body. Receiving compassion makes you stronger: more able to take a breath, find your footing, and keep on going.

You get the benefits of both giving and receiving compassion when you offer it to yourself. Much as you can see the burdens and stresses of others, you can recognize these same things in yourself. Much as you can feel moved by their suffering, you can be touched by your own. You can bring the same support to yourself that you'd provide for someone else. And if there's not much compassion for you coming from others, it's more important than ever to give it to yourself.

This is *not* whining or wallowing in misery. Compassion for yourself is where you start when things are tough, not where you stop. Research by Kristin Neff and others has shown that self-compassion makes a person more resilient, more able to bounce back. It lowers self-criticism and builds up self-worth, helping you to be more ambitious and successful, not complacent and lazy. In compassion for your own pain is a sense of common humanity: we all suffer, we all face disease and death, we all lose others we love. Everyone is fragile. As Leonard Cohen sang: "There is a crack in everything / That's how the light gets in." Everyone is cracked. Everyone needs compassion.

Challenges to Self-Compassion

Yet self-compassion is challenging for many of us. One reason has to do with how our nervous system works. The brain is designed to be changed by our experiences, particularly *negative* ones, and especially those that occurred in childhood. It's normal to internalize the ways that your parents and others have treated you—which might have included ignoring, belittling, or punishing your softer feelings and longings—and then treat yourself in the same way.

For example, I had conscientious and loving parents, and I'm very grateful to them. That said, while growing up, I experienced frequent criticism and not much compassion, and I took these attitudes into myself. I've always been moved by the pain of others. But my own pain? I pushed it away, and then wondered why it kept growing.

Learning Compassion

I had to learn how to bring compassion to my own suffering. We learn many things in life, including how to ride a bicycle, apologize to a friend, or talk ourselves down from being upset. What does it take for learning to happen?

The key to growing any psychological resource, including compassion, is to have repeated experiences of it *that get turned into lasting changes in neural structure or function*. It's like recording a song on an old-fashioned tape recorder: as the song plays—as you experience the resource—you can help it leave a physical trace behind in your nervous system.

When you're already experiencing something enjoyable or useful—perhaps the satisfaction in finishing a report at work or the comfort in plopping onto the sofa at the end of a long day—simply *notice* it. You can also deliberately *create* an experience of something you want to develop, such as the feeling of being on your own side. Once you're having the experience, feel it as fully as possible and take a little time—a breath or two or ten—to stay with it. The more often you do this, the more you will tend to hardwire psychological resources into yourself.

To develop more self-compassion, take a few minutes to try the practice in the box. As you build up compassion for yourself, you'll be more able to tap into it whenever you want.

COMPASSION FOR YOURSELF

Bring to mind times you have felt cared about by people, pets, or spiritual beings, in your life today or in your past. Any kind of caring for you counts, such as times you were included, seen, appreciated, liked, or loved. Relax and open yourself to feeling cared about. If you get distracted, just come back to feeling cared about. Stay with these feelings and sense them sinking in, like water into a sponge.

Then think about one or more people you have compassion for—perhaps a child in pain, a friend going through a divorce, or refugees on the other side of the world. Get a sense of their burdens, worries, and suffering. Feel a warmheartedness, a sympathetic concern. You could put a hand on your heart and have thoughts such as, "May your pain ease . . . may you find work . . . may you get through this illness." Give yourself over to compassion, letting it fill you and flow through you.

Knowing what compassion feels like, apply it to yourself. Recognize any ways you feel stressed, tired, ill, mistreated, or unhappy. Then bring compassion to yourself as you would to a friend who felt like you do. Know that everyone suffers and that you are not alone in your pain. Perhaps place a hand on your heart or your cheek. Depending on what has happened, you could think, "May I not suffer . . . may these hurt feelings pass . . . may I not worry so much . . . may I heal from this illness." Imagine compassion like a gentle warm rain coming down into you, touching and soothing the weary, hurting, longing places inside.

FIND ACCEPTANCE

One time a friend and I climbed the East Buttress to the top of Mount Whitney. The route back to our tent went down a snow-filled gulley. It was October, the snow had turned to ice, and we had to move carefully and slowly. It was getting dark and we couldn't see where we were going. Rather than risk a deadly fall, we decided to sit on a small ledge all night, wrapped in a space blanket with our feet in our daypacks, shivering in freezing temperatures.

I didn't like being there but had to face the reality of our situation. Denying it or fighting it could have killed us. High on that mountain, taking care of myself had to include recognizing and accepting whatever was true about the world around me. Acceptance can sit alongside other reactions. For example, a person can be outraged by an injustice and accept that it's a reality. Acceptance doesn't mean complacency or giving up. We can accept something while at the same time trying to make it better.

I also needed to accept what was happening inside me. I was tired and cold and worried. That's how I felt. Trying to push these feelings away would have added stress to an already stressful situation and made me feel worse. Sometimes it is skillful to nudge thoughts and feelings in a healthier, happier direction. But that only works if we accept our reactions in the first place. Otherwise, our nudging has little traction, and we're just putting a false face on how we really feel. If we don't accept what's true about ourselves, we won't see it clearly, and if we don't see it clearly, we'll be less able to deal with it.

The whole self is like a big house, and not accepting all of who you are is like closing up some of its rooms: "Uh-oh, can't look vulnerable, better shut that door." "Asking for love made me look like a fool, never again with that, lock it up." "I make mistakes when I get excited, so that's it with passion, throw away the key." What would it be like to open all the doors inside yourself? You can still keep an eye on what lies inside the various rooms, and decide what you act upon or show to the world. Accepting what's inside yourself gives you more influence over it, not less. Try the practice in the box to deepen your sense of this.

SELF-ACCEPTANCE

Look around and find something that exists—and accept it. Know what it feels like to accept something.

Think about a friend, and different aspects of this person. Explore what it's like to accept these aspects of your friend. See if you can feel an easing, opening, and calming as a result.

Be aware of your experience. Try to accept whatever you are experiencing without adding anything to it. Can you accept the sensations of breathing as they are? If judgments come up, can you accept these, too? Try saying little things to yourself like "I accept this thought" or "I accept this pain" or "I accept that I feel grateful—or sad." If there is resistance to something, can you accept that resistance? If certain parts of your experience are challenging, recall the sense of being on your own side and the feeling of self-compassion. Be aware of acceptance as an experience itself, an attitude or orientation toward things that sees without turning away, that receives without resisting. Let acceptance spread inside you.

Be aware of different parts of yourself, ones you like and ones you don't. You could name some to yourself: "There is a part that enjoys sweets . . . a part that is lonely . . . a part that is critical . . .

a part that feels young . . . a part that wants love." Then explore accepting the fact of these parts, beginning with the easier ones. If certain things are hard to accept, that's normal and all right, and you can come back to them later if you want. You could say to yourself things like "I accept the part of me that loves my children . . . I accept the part of me that leaves dishes in the sink . . . I accept the part of me that was bullied in school . . . I accept the part of me that is resentful." Acceptance could feel like a softening inside, an opening to and including of various parts of yourself. You might put your arms around yourself, embracing all of you. Sink into self-acceptance as it sinks into you.

ENJOY LIFE

If a drug company could patent enjoyment, there would be ads for it every night on TV. Enjoyable experiences—such as petting a cat, drinking water when you're thirsty, or smiling at a friend—lower stress hormones, strengthen the immune system, and help you settle back down if you've gotten frustrated or worried.

As enjoyment increases, so does the activity of key neurochemicals, including *dopamine*, *norepinephrine*, and *natural opioids*. Deep in the brain, circuits in the *basal ganglia* use rising dopamine to prioritize and pursue actions that feel rewarding. If you'd like to be more motivated about certain things—such as exercising, eating healthy foods, or pushing through a tough project at work—focusing on what's enjoyable about them will naturally draw you into doing them. Norepinephrine helps you stay alert and engaged. In a boring afternoon meeting, finding something, anything, to enjoy about it will keep you awake and make you more effective. Natural opioids, including endorphins, calm your body if you're stressed and reduce physical and emotional pain.

Together, dopamine and norepinephrine flag experiences as

"keepers," heightening their consolidation as lasting resources inside your brain. Let's say you'd like to be more patient at home or work. To grow this inner strength, look for opportunities to experience some patience. Then focus on whatever is enjoyable about it, such as how good it feels to stay calm and relaxed. An experience of patience or any other psychological resource is a *state* of mind, and enjoying it helps turn it into a positive *trait* embedded in your brain.

Enjoying life is a powerful way to care for yourself. Think about some of the things you enjoy. For me, they include smelling coffee, talking with my kids, and seeing a blade of grass push up through a crack in a sidewalk. What's on your own list? Not so much the million-dollar moments, but the small real opportunities for enjoyment present in even the toughest life: perhaps feeling friendly with someone, relaxing when you exhale, or drifting to sleep at the end of a long hard day. And no matter what is happening outside you, you can always find something to enjoy inside your own mind: maybe a private joke, an imagined experience, or recognizing your own warm heart.

These small ways to enjoy the life that you have contain a big lesson. It's usually the little things adding up over time that make the largest difference. There is a saying in Tibet: "If you take care of the minutes, the years will take care of themselves."

What's the most important minute in life? I think it's the next one. There is nothing we can do about the past, and we have limited influence over the hours and days to come. But the next minute—minute after minute after minute—is always full of possibility. Are there opportunities to be on your own side, bring caring to your pain, accept yourself, and enjoy what you can? Is there something you could heal, something you could learn?

Minute by minute, step by step, strength after strength, you can always grow more of the good inside yourself. For your own sake, and the sake of others as well.

KEY POINTS

- Compassion involves warmhearted concern for suffering and the desire to relieve it if you can. Compassion can be given both to others and to yourself.

- Compassion is a psychological resource—an inner strength—that can be developed over time. We grow inner strengths by having experiences of them that lead to lasting changes in the nervous system.

- Getting on your own side and bringing caring to your pain will make you more resilient, confident, and capable. Being good to yourself is good for others, too.

- Accepting things as they are—including yourself—helps you deal with them more effectively, and with less resistance and stress.

- Enjoyable moments enrich each day. They also lower stress, connect you with others, and increase your learning—the lasting benefit—from the experiences you're having.

- Little things add up over time. Many times a day, you can change your brain for the better.

CHAPTER 2

MINDFULNESS

*The education of attention would be
the education par excellence.*

—William James

Being mindful means staying present in this moment as it is, moment after moment, rather than daydreaming, ruminating, or being distracted. The sustained present-moment awareness of mindfulness is easy—for maybe a breath or two in a row. The key is to *stay* mindful—which, as much research has shown, lowers stress, protects health, and lifts mood.

It's pretty easy to be mindful while sitting on a cushion, a cup of warm tea in hand. It's harder to stay mindful when things are stressful or emotionally demanding, such as while having an argument with someone you love. Mindfulness can feel most out of reach just when you need it the most.

To build the strength of mindfulness, we'll start with practical ways to develop stable and steady attention, and to center yourself so that you're not distracted or hijacked by stressful or upsetting experiences. Next, we'll explore the three major ways to relate to and guide your own mind, and the role of mindfulness in each of these. Then we'll see how to use mindfulness to take care of the basic needs we all have: to be safe, satisfied, and connected. In the final section, we'll explore the two different ways the brain deals with challenging conditions, and how mindfulness can help you respond to them with an underlying sense of peace, contentment, and love instead of reacting to them from a place of fear, frustration, and hurt.

STEADY THE MIND

Your nervous system is designed to be changed by your experiences—the technical term for this is *experience-dependent neuroplasticity*—and your experiences depend on what you're paying attention to. There's an old saying: "You become what you eat." That's true for the body, but *you*—the person you are—gradually become what your attention rests upon. Can you keep your attention on the many things that are useful and enjoyable in your day, drawing them into yourself? Or do you get preoccupied with worries, self-criticism, and resentments, making these a part of yourself?

In order to convert passing experiences into lasting inner strengths, we have to be able to focus attention on an experience long enough for it to start being consolidated into the nervous system. Unfortunately, most of us have skittery attention, with a mind that is darting and wandering this way and that. There are a variety of reasons. We live in a revved-up, media-bombarding, multitasking, stimulation-chasing culture. Personal stress, anxiety, depression, and trauma can make it harder to focus. And some people are just more naturally distractible than others are.

How Mindfulness Works

Mindfulness is the key to regulating your attention so that you get the most out of beneficial experiences while limiting the impact of stressful, harmful ones. It enables you to recognize where your attention has gone. The root of the word for mindfulness in Pali, the language of early Buddhism, refers to *memory*. With mindfulness, you are recollected rather than forgetful, collected and gathered together rather than scattered apart.

You can be mindful of what is in a narrow field of attention, such as getting a thread through the eye of a needle, or a very broad one, such as observing the whole ongoing stream of consciousness. And you can apply mindful awareness to both your inner and outer world, such as hurt feelings inside when somebody lets you down or a truck driving next to your car in the rain.

Other things could be happening alongside mindfulness, such as compassion for your hurt feelings or caution about a truck getting too close on a busy highway, but mindfulness itself does not try to change your experience or behavior. It is receptive and accepting, not judging or directing. Mindfulness holds your reactions in a spacious awareness that is itself never disturbed by whatever passes through it. With mindfulness, you can step back from your reactions and observe them from a more peaceful and centered place. You can accept them for what they are while at the same time not being identified with them. Of course, this does not mean that the only way to be mindful is to passively witness your experiences rolling by. You can be mindful while also talking with others, making choices, and accomplishing one thing after another.

Strengthening Mindfulness

Mindfulness is a kind of mental muscle, and you can strengthen it by making it a regular part of daily life. Over time, developing a continuity of mindfulness will give you a quality of sustained presence that is grounded and unwavering.

BE MINDFUL OF BEING MINDFUL

Have you ever been lost in some mental reverie, such as worrying about money or what a friend thinks of you, and then felt like you "woke up" from it? This is an experience of mindfulness. You might also have a sense of present-moment awareness while walking to work, pausing to look out the window, or reflecting on your day as you get ready for bed.

Whenever you experience it, know what mindfulness feels like. You have come home to yourself. You are simply here, simply now . . . steadily. Also be mindful of *not* being mindful. Try to get faster at noticing when your attention wanders. For example, you could set your phone to chime softly at random times to remind you to be mindful throughout your day. With a little practice, you will already be centered in the present moment the next time the chime sounds.

REDUCE DISTRACTIONS

You could also use your phone's "do not disturb" feature to reduce texts and calls that interrupt you. In a sense, your attention is your property. As best you can, don't let other people or the rushing world around you take it from you without your permission. Try to slow down and do one thing at a time with your full attention.

WEAVE MINDFULNESS INTO YOUR DAY

Tune into your breathing while talking with others or doing tasks. This will help you stay grounded in yourself and in the present moment. Return to an awareness of your breathing many, many times a day. You can use regular events such as meals to pause, collect yourself, and come into the present. And you can strengthen your attention by doing something you like, such as a craft or a crossword puzzle, that requires concentration.

MEDITATE

There are many methods, traditions, and teachers of meditation, in both secular forms and prayer. People ask, "What is the best meditation?" I think the best meditation is the one that a person will actually, consistently, do. So find what is enjoyable and effective for you. You could commit to meditating a minute or more each day—even if it's the last minute before your head hits the pillow. I've made this commitment myself, and honestly, it changed my life. I began meditating in 1974 and have found that the most powerful meditations are usually the simplest, and I suggest that you try the one in the box.

A SIMPLE MEDITATION

Set aside a few minutes or more in a quiet place. Find a comfortable posture while sitting, standing, or lying down. Or you could walk slowly, perhaps back and forth in a room. Focus on something that will help you stay present, such as a sensation, a word, an image, or a feeling. Here I'll use the breath; adapt my suggestions if you use another object of attention.

Be aware of the sensations of breathing in your face, chest, stomach, or body in general. Apply attention to the beginning of an inhalation, sustain awareness over the course of it, and then apply and sustain attention to the exhalation . . . breath after breath. If it helps, in the back of your mind count each full breath up to four or perhaps ten, and start over again; if you lose track of the count, just start over with one. Or use soft words to yourself, such as "in . . . out . . . rising . . . falling." If your mind wanders, that's normal; when you notice it, simply return to your object of attention.

As you breathe, relax. Sounds and thoughts, memories and feelings, will come and go, passing through awareness. You are not trying to silence your mind. Rather, you are disengaging from distractions, neither resisting things that are unpleasant nor following after things that are pleasant. You are settling into simply being in the present, letting go of the past and not fearing or planning the future. Nothing to fix, no other place to go, no one you have to be. Rest and relax as a whole body breathing.

Without strain or stress, see if you can open to a growing peacefulness. Then at your own pace, see if you can find a sense of contentment. And when you like, open to a feeling of love. Other things may be present in awareness, such as pain or worry, and that's all right. Let them be while you remain aware of the breath, perhaps with a growing sense of overall well-being.

During the meditation, feel relaxation and other beneficial experiences sinking into you, becoming a part of you. As you approach the end of this practice, let yourself really receive whatever has been beneficial in it.

FIND REFUGE

Mindfulness helps you open up to the deeper layers of yourself. Usually this feels pretty good. But sometimes, if you're not ready for it, it can feel like opening a trapdoor to uncomfortable and frightening material. For example, when I started college at the tail end of the 1960s, people would say, "Hey man, feel your feelings, experience your experience." I thought they were crazy. My feelings hurt. Why would I want to feel them? Still, I knew I had to open up. But it sure was scary. I needed a way to feel safe no matter what came up out of the trapdoor. I needed to find *refuge*.

I thought back to when I was a child and would slip out of our house and walk into the orange groves and hills nearby. Climbing trees and being outdoors helped me relax and feel strong. I carried those good feelings back with me when I returned to my home, as if the trees and hills were inside me and I could go to them in my mind for comfort and support. Years later in college, I went back to that feeling of refuge I'd found in nature, and it helped me be brave enough to explore the dark and spooky basement of my mind—which was rarely as painful as I'd feared.

Knowing Your Refuges

A refuge is anything that protects, nurtures, or uplifts you. Life can be hard, and everyone has difficult, uncomfortable experiences. We all need refuges. What are your own?

A pet or other people could be a refuge for you. My wife is a refuge for me, and Forrest's friends are a refuge for him. Places can be refuges, such as a favorite coffee shop, or a church, library, or park. Certain things can feel like a refuge, such as a cup of coffee, a cozy sweater, or a good book at the end of a long day. You might also find refuge in different activities—perhaps walking the dog, playing your guitar, or watching some TV before bed.

Some refuges are intangible. Memories of being outdoors have been important refuges for me, from the orange trees of my childhood to trips in deep wilderness as an adult. You might remember the feeling of your grandmother's kitchen, or of your own grandson falling asleep in your lap. For many people, the sense of something sacred or divine is a profound refuge. Ideas can be refuges, such as the discoveries of scientists or the wisdom of saints—or simply knowing that your children do in fact love you.

As well, there is the key refuge of having faith in whatever is good inside yourself. This doesn't mean overlooking the rest. You're simply seeing your decency, warmth and kindness, good intentions, capabilities, and efforts. These are facts about you, and recognizing them is a reliable source of refuge.

Using Your Refuges

In the flow of your day, find refuges such as time to yourself in a morning shower, the friendly camaraderie of people at work, listening to music on the way home, or thoughts of gratitude as you get ready for sleep. You can also set aside some time to create sustained experiences of refuge, such as through the practice in the box.

When you find a refuge, slow down. Be aware of what that refuge feels like: perhaps a sense of relaxation, reassurance, and relief. Stay with the experience for a breath or longer. Notice what feels good about it. Let the sense of refuge sink in, establishing itself in you as something you can go to whenever you want.

If you're being mindful and start to feel overwhelmed by whatever is coming up into awareness, focus on a refuge and the feeling it gives you. It's like standing inside a sheltered place looking out at a storm. Eventually the storm will pass, as all experiences do, and the peaceful intact core of you will remain.

TAKING REFUGE

Pick something that is a refuge for you, such as the image of a beautiful meadow, the memory of a loved one, or the wisdom in a saying. Open to feelings and sensations related to this refuge. Get a sense of having a refuge, and stay with this experience and let it in.

Try naming the refuge to yourself, such as "I take refuge in _____." See how this feels, and allow the sense of refuge to grow inside you. Try this naming with other refuges.

Explore relating to a refuge not as something "over there" that's separate from you, but rather as something already present in you. You could say to yourself things like "May I come from _____ ," or "I'm abiding as _____ ," or "May I be uplifted by _____ ." Regarded in this way, a refuge can feel like a wholesome, beneficial current carrying you along.

Try taking refuge in gratitude . . . in the feeling of being liked by people who do care about you . . . in the sense of your kindness and decency . . . in anything else you want.

Give over to your refuges. Let them live you.

LET BE, LET GO, LET IN

Clinical psychology, coaching, human resources training, personal growth workshops, and the world's contemplative traditions offer many different ways to be happy, loving, effective, and wise. But for all the variety in these approaches and methods, they cluster into three groups, three major ways to engage your mind.

First, you can *be with what's there*. Feel the feelings, experience the experience, the bitter as well as the sweet. You could explore an experience's different aspects—such as the sensations in it, as well as emotions, thoughts, and desires—and perhaps down to more vulnerable material, like the hurt often found beneath anger. In the process of being with it, an experience might change, but you are not deliberately trying to change it.

Second, you can *decrease the negative*—whatever is painful or harmful—by preventing, reducing, or ending it. For example, you could vent feelings to a friend, step away from self-critical thoughts, stop bringing home cookies that fuel desires for sugar, or ease tension by relaxing your body.

Third, you can *increase the positive*—whatever is enjoyable or beneficial—by creating, growing, or preserving it. You could breathe more quickly to lift your energy, remember times with friends that make you feel happy, have realistic and useful thoughts about a situation at work, or motivate yourself by imagining how good it will feel to eat healthy foods.

In other words, getting good at coping, healing, and well-being is a matter of getting good at *letting be*, *letting go*, and *letting in*. Mindfulness is necessary for all of these, since we can't let be, let go, or let in without it. Also, these ways to practice with the mind work together. For example, you could use the third one—increasing the positive—to grow an inner resource such as self-compassion in order to be with painful feelings.

Imagine that your mind is a garden. You can tend to it in three ways: observe it, pull weeds, and plant flowers. Observing it is fundamental, and sometimes that's all you can do. Perhaps something terrible has happened and you can only ride out the storm. But being with the mind is not enough; we must work with it as well. The mind is grounded in the brain, which is a physical system that doesn't change for the better on its own. Weeds don't get pulled and flowers don't get planted simply by watching the garden.

Moving Through an Upset

The three ways to engage the mind provide a step-by-step road map for moving through an upset. Suppose you feel stressed, hurt, or angry. Start by being with whatever is happening inside you. Tune into your body, perhaps your chest tightening or a sinking feeling in your stomach. Explore your emotions, thoughts, and desires. Also look for what might be deeper and more vulnerable, such as the pain of a recent break-up beneath worries about dating again. Try to accept your experience as it is without resisting it, even if it's uncomfortable. Be on your own side and have compassion for yourself.

Second, when it feels right, move into letting go. Take a few breaths while exhaling slowly and let any tension drain out of your body. As appropriate, you can release emotions by venting to a friend, yelling in the shower, crying, or imagining a river of light pouring through you and washing away any sad or upsetting feelings. Pull your attention away from negative thought loops. Challenge beliefs that are exaggerated or untrue by thinking of reasons why they are wrong. Try to see the big picture. Whatever has happened is probably a short chapter in the long book of your life. Know how a problematic desire—such as wanting to lash out in anger—could hurt you or others. Imagine holding that desire in your hand like a stone and then dropping it.

Third, when you're ready, shift to letting in. Recognize that you've come through something hard, and appreciate yourself for doing so. Let easing and relaxing spread through your body. Notice or bring to mind feelings that are natural replacements for what you have released, such as reassurance spreading inside as anxiety leaves. Focus on thoughts that are accurate and useful, replacing those that are wrong and harmful. See if there are any lessons to learn, such as ways to be kinder to yourself or more effective with others. Decide if there is anything to do differently from now on, such as leaving earlier for the airport or not talking about money with your partner right before going to sleep.

Trust your intuition about when to move from one step to the next. It's like the story of Goldilocks and the Three Bears, in which one bed was too hard, one was too soft, and one was just right. What feels "just right" will depend on the experience itself. For example, you could be with a judgmental thought for a few seconds and recognize its familiar yapping ("Oh, there it is again, ranting about how others drive"), and then shift quickly to letting go. There is no value in listening to it rattle on and on; you already got the message, so you hang up the phone.

But sometimes things are just really hard and the most you can do is simply bear them. Perhaps your partner has died, and it takes years to move through the first and second steps—letting be and letting go—before you can even imagine letting someone else into your heart. Other people may want to hurry you along, but go at your own pace. Maybe all you can do is touch the pain for a few seconds, and then you need to back away from it for a while before being with it again. Personally, I entered adulthood with a big bucket of tears deep inside. Feeling it all at once would have been overwhelming, so I've gradually emptied it one spoonful at a time.

If you try to let go and let in but find that it feels superficial or inauthentic, go back to the first step and be with your mind. Explore what else is there to experience fully, perhaps something softer and younger. The process of letting be, letting go, and letting in can sometimes uncover the next layer of psychological material. Then you can use the three steps to move through that layer, and perhaps additional layers, in a deepening spiral. Stay mindful, and you'll be pulling weeds, planting flowers, and getting to know your garden better all along the way.

TAKE CARE OF YOUR NEEDS

Soon after Forrest was born, my parents came to visit, and my mother was excited to hold her first grandchild. She perched him on her chest close to her face and bubbled away, "Oh, what a sweet baby, what a good baby you are!" But he couldn't hold up his head to look at her, and he started fussing. My mother kept talking to him while he became more and more upset. I murmured, "Uh, Mom, I think he wants you to hold him to the side so he's more comfortable." She said happily, "He doesn't know what he wants." Startled, I said he did want to be held differently, since he'd been fine until she picked him up. She replied with cheerful gusto, "Oh, who cares what he wants!" I muttered that I did and retrieved our son.

There's a lot in this story. My mother was a very loving person, and ecstatic about seeing Forrest. She was just expressing two beliefs that had guided how she was brought up: children are not really beings who know what they want, and even if they do, their wants don't matter much compared to those of adults.

Realistically, no child or adult can have every want satisfied every time. Nor should they, since some desires are harmful. Still, at the bottom of every want is a healthy need. My mom needed to feel close to her family; she needed to give love and have it received; she needed to feel that she mattered and was respected. These are completely normal needs. Excited to see us and raised in a certain way herself, she went about meeting her needs in ways that were problematic—unskillful with a baby and insensitive to her son and daughter-in-law—but her underlying intentions were good.

Needs and wants blur together, and what is a need to one person could be a want to someone else, so I'm not going to draw a sharp line between them. Every living creature—including a big, complicated human one—is motivated to pursue its wants and satisfy its needs. Wanting is fundamental and inescapable. Consequently, a deepening awareness of your wants and needs—and your thoughts and feelings *about* them—can help you meet them more effectively and accept yourself more fully.

Learning About Wanting

Be mindful of your experiences related to wanting. These experiences include preferring one thing over another, pursuing a goal, making a request, and insisting on something. In particular, notice how you're affected by the reactions of others to your wants and needs. If they're supportive, that probably feels good. But if they ignore, dismiss, or thwart you, it's natural to feel that your wants and needs don't matter and could in fact be embarrassing, even disgusting—and by extension, that *you* don't matter, and that there could be something wrong with you, something you ought to suppress and hide.

The residues of these and other experiences are stored in the brain, as emotional, social, and somatic *learning.* This begins when we are very young, and very dependent on others to read our wants and needs accurately and respond to them kindly and effectively. We learn about wanting itself: which wants are allowed and can be pursued directly, which ones are supposed to be camouflaged and sought covertly, and which ones are considered shameful and must be denied.

With mindfulness, you can look inside and understand yourself better. Take a little time, and explore the answers to these questions:

- How did your parents respond to your wants? What did you learn about wanting while growing up?

- As an adult, how have others responded to your wants? In what ways have you been supported? In what ways have your wants been ignored, criticized, or defeated? How have you felt about all this?

- How has your past affected how you go about meeting your wants and needs these days? For example, have you been embarrassed about some of the things you want?

- Reflecting on all this, are there are any changes you'd like to make? Perhaps you could be more open about something you want, or more straightforward about seeking it.

Your Three Needs

Mindfulness of your past helps you to know yourself better in the present, and to be more effective at taking care of your needs in the future. So, what do you need? Psychological theories classify needs in various ways. As a summary of these ideas, I've categorized them into three basic needs:

1. We need *safety*, from raw survival to knowing we won't be attacked if we speak up. We fulfill this need by *avoiding* harms, such as not touching a hot stove or steering clear of certain people.

2. We need *satisfaction*, from having enough to eat to feeling that life is worth living. We handle this by *approaching* rewards, such as smelling the roses, finishing the laundry, or building a business.

3. We need *connection*, from expressing sexuality to feeling worthy and loved. We take care of this need by *attaching* to others, such as by texting a friend, feeling understood, or giving compassion.

Every animal species, including human beings, needs its version of safety, satisfaction, and connection. These basic needs are grounded in life itself, and how we manage them today is based on the evolution of the nervous system over the past 600 million years. To simplify a long, complex process, the brain has been built from the bottom up, like a house with three floors.

In the "house" of the brain, the first and oldest floor is the *brain stem*, developed during the reptilian stage of evolution, with a focus on safety: in its essence the most fundamental need of all, to stay alive. The second floor is the *subcortex*, which contains the *hypothalamus*, *thalamus*, *amygdala*, *hippocampus*, and *basal ganglia*. This part of your brain has taken shape during the mammalian phase of evolution, which began around 200 million years ago. The subcortex helps us be more effective in pursuing satisfaction. The top floor is the *neocortex*, which started expanding with the first primates about 50 million years ago; it has tripled in volume since early hominids began manufacturing tools 2.5 million years ago. The neocortex has enabled humans to be the most social species on the planet. It is the neural basis of empathy, language, cooperative planning, and compassion—sophisticated ways to meet our needs for connection.

In a sense, we're walking around with a zoo inside our heads. Solutions to life-or-death problems faced by our ancient ancestors while swimming in dark oceans, hiding from dinosaurs, or fighting with other Stone Age bands are built into the brain today. While the parts of the brain work together to meet our needs, they do have specialized functions shaped by our evolutionary history. To push the metaphor, it's as if we each have an inner lizard freezing or fleeing from danger, a mouse sniffing about for cheese, and a monkey looking for its tribe.

Embracing Your Needs

It can feel embarrassing to admit that you have needs. A country or culture may value rugged independence, but the reality is that we all depend on many things for survival, success, and happiness, from the air we breathe to the kindness of strangers to the infrastructure of civilization. Real ruggedness is being brave enough to admit the fact of ordinary human neediness.

A healthy body and mind do not come from denying, "overcoming," or transcending needs. They are instead the natural result of taking care of your needs, and being mindful of the needs of others. Consequently, it's the needs we push away that are often the most important to embrace.

So try to be aware of needs, or aspects of needs, that have been unmet. Listen to the longings of your heart. As you go through your day, be mindful of your needs for:

- **Safety.** Notice when you feel uneasy, irritated, or over-whelmed. See if any beliefs that may not actually be true are making you anxious. When it feels right, shift into letting go and letting in, such as finding refuges and settling as best you can into a place of peace.

- **Satisfaction.** Be aware of any feelings of boredom, disappointment, frustration, or loss. After you've explored this experience, you could think of things you're grateful for or glad about. See if you can find a sense of contentment.

- **Connection.** Notice when you feel hurt, resentment, envy, loneliness, or inadequacy. Then recall times when you felt cared about—and times when you felt friendly or caring yourself. Rest in love flowing in and flowing out.

RESPONDING OR REACTING

Life challenges our needs all the time. But we can experience that our needs are met even as we take practical steps to cope with intense challenges. For example, I've been in many dangerous places while rock-climbing, standing on little edges the width of a pencil with a long fall if I slipped. My need for safety was definitely challenged at these times. But inside I almost always felt completely safe. I'd climbed a lot and felt comfortable doing it, and knew I was tied in to a rope with a capable partner holding the other end. I was on high alert, cautious and wary, dealing with intense threats—and usually having the time of my life.

You probably have your own examples of calmly managing and even enjoying very challenging activities or situations. Life is turbulent and unpredictable, containing wonderful opportunities that still take a lot of work and inevitable losses and pains. We can't avoid challenges. The only question is how we deal with them. There is a fundamental difference between facing challenges while experiencing that your needs are being sufficiently met, and facing challenges while experiencing that your needs are *not* being met.

Green Zone, Red Zone

When we experience that needs are sufficiently met, there is a sense of *fullness* and *balance*. The body and the mind default to their resting state, which I call the Responsive mode, or "green zone." The body conserves its resources, refuels and repairs itself, and recovers from stress. In the mind, there is a sense of *peace*, *contentment*, and *love*—broad, umbrella terms related to our needs for safety, satisfaction, and connection. This is embodied well-being.

On the other hand, when we experience that a need is unmet, there is a sense of *deficit* and *disturbance*: something missing, something wrong. The body and the mind are agitated out of their resting state into the Reactive mode, or "red zone." The body fires up into fight, flight, or freeze reactions, shaking up its immune, hormonal, cardiovascular, and digestive systems. In the mind, there is a sense of *fear*, *frustration*, and *hurt*—umbrella terms related to our needs for safety, satisfaction, and connection. This is stress, distress, and dysfunction.

The distinction between the Responsive and Reactive modes is inherently fuzzy. Still, we all know the difference between feeling capable and confident while handling a challenge or feeling rattled and worried. Here is a summary of these two modes.

MEETING OUR NEEDS

Need	Met By	Brain	Evolution	Responsive	Reactive
Safety	Avoiding	Brain stem	Reptile	Peace	Fear
Satisfaction	Approaching	Subcortex	Mammal	Contentment	Frustration
Connection	Attaching	Neocortex	Primate/ Human	Love	Hurt

It's possible to experience that one basic need is unmet while the other two are doing fine. For example, two parents could feel emotionally disconnected from their rebellious adolescent while at the same time knowing that they are all physically safe and able to pursue opportunities for rewards in other areas. When one need "goes red" while the others "stay green," then reactions to the unmet need can spread to involve other needs; in this example, the parents might start to feel anxious about the teenager's safety and frustrated about the goal of getting their child through high school. Alternately, feeling resourced in other areas can help address a particular need that's blinking red; the parents here could draw on a sense of their commitment to the teen's safety and the knowledge that they do have effective ways to satisfy the requirements of high school. Sometimes all you can do is preserve a tiny little green refuge in yourself that stays calm and strong while the rest of you is upset. But the sense of that small sanctuary makes a great difference, and with time you can gradually move out from it to ease and take care of the rest of your mind.

The Responsive and Reactive modes are not just the result of experiencing that needs are met or unmet. They are also two different *ways* to meet our needs. To borrow an example from Robert Sapolsky's book *Why Zebras Don't Get Ulcers*, imagine being a zebra in a large herd in Africa. You're eating grass, keeping a watchful eye out for lions but staying calm, interacting with other zebras, and enjoying yourself as you handle your needs from the Responsive mode. Suddenly some lions attack, and your herd bursts into a Reactive mode flight of panicky activity that ends quickly . . . one way or another. And then you and the other zebras return to Responsive ways of handling life on the savannah.

In a nutshell, this is Mother Nature's blueprint: long periods of Responsive mode management of needs punctuated by occasional spikes *when necessary* of Reactive mode stress followed by rapid recovery back to the green zone. The Responsive mode feels good because it *is* good: the body is protected and replenished, and the mind is at ease and content. On the other hand, the Reactive mode feels bad because it *is* bad, especially over the long run: the body becomes disturbed and depleted, and the mind becomes occupied by anxiety, irritation, disappointment, hurt, and resentment.

The Reactive mode tears us down, while the Responsive mode builds us up. Adversity is certainly an opportunity to develop resilience, *stress-hardiness*, and even *post-traumatic growth*. But for a person to grow through adversity, there must also be Responsive resources present such as determination and sense of purpose. Plus most opportunities in daily life to experience and develop mental resources do not involve adversity: there is simply a moment of relaxation, gratitude, enthusiasm, self-worth, or kindness. Meanwhile, most moments of fear, frustration, or hurt are simply unpleasant and stressful, with no benefit left behind. Adversity is to be faced and learned from, but I think people sometimes overrate its value. On the whole, Reactive experiences make us more brittle and fragile over time, while Responsive experiences tend to make us more resilient.

The Reactive mode evolved to be a brief solution to immediate threats to survival—not a way of life. Unfortunately, while we're no longer running from saber-toothed tigers, our modern multitasking, racing about, and frequent stresses keep pushing us into the red zone. Then it's hard to leave due to what researchers call the brain's *negativity bias*.

The Negativity Bias

Our ancestors needed to gain "carrots" such as food and sex, and to escape from "sticks" such as predators and aggression inside or between their bands. Both are important, but sticks usually have more urgency and impact for survival. Back on the Serengeti plains, if you failed to get a carrot, you'd still have a chance to get another one, but if you failed to avoid a stick—*whack*, no more carrots forever.

As a result, the brain naturally and routinely:

1. Scans for bad news out in the world and inside the body and mind

2. Focuses tightly on it, losing sight of the big picture

3. Overreacts to it

4. Fast-tracks the experience into emotional, somatic, and social memory

5. Becomes sensitized through repeated doses of the stress hormone cortisol, so it becomes even more reactive to negative experiences—which bathe the brain in even more cortisol, creating a vicious cycle

In effect, our brains are like Velcro for bad experiences but Teflon for good ones. For example, if ten things happen to you during a day at work or in a relationship, and nine of them are positive while one is negative, what do you tend to think about most? Probably the negative one. Pleasant, useful, beneficial experiences happen many times a day—enjoying a cup of coffee, getting something done at home or work, snuggling into bed with a good book at night—but they ordinarily pass through the brain like water through a sieve, while each stressful or harmful experience gets stuck to it. We're designed to over-learn from bad experiences while under-learning from good ones. The negativity bias made sense for survival over millions of years of evolution, but today it's a kind of universal learning disability in a brain designed for peak performance under Stone Age conditions.

The effects of this bias are worsened by the recent evolution of neural networks in the midline of the cortex that enable *mental time travel*: reflecting on the past and planning for the future. These networks also enable *negative rumination*. Unlike our animal cousins, who learn from their close calls but don't obsess about them, we tend to keep going over worries, resentments, and self-criticism: "So many things could go wrong." "How dare they treat me that way?" "I am such an idiot!" The thoughts and feelings we have while ruminating change the brain just as other negative experiences do. Running these loops repeatedly is like running laps in soft dirt, deepening the track each time we go around it—which makes it easier to fall into negative rumination in the future.

COMING HOME, STAYING HOME

To sum it up, we have no choice about our three needs, or how the reptilian-mammalian-primate stages of evolution have shaped the ways that the brain tries to meet our needs. Our only choice is *how* we meet our needs: from the green zone or the red zone, with an underlying sense of peace, contentment, and love, or with a sense of fear, frustration, and hurt.

The Responsive mode is our home base, a healthy equilibrium of body and mind. It's the essence of well-being and the basis of sustained resilience. But we're easily driven from that home and into the red zone. Then, it's easy to get stuck there due to the negativity bias and negative rumination, in a kind of chronic inner homelessness.

It's not our fault we're like this. It's our biological endowment, a gift of sorts from Mother Nature. But there is a lot we can do about it.

Leave the Red Zone

Sometimes it's necessary to meet challenges in Reactive ways. Maybe you have to dodge a car coming at you or fire up to deal with someone who's getting way too aggressive. Humans are tough, and we can tolerate trips to the red zone. But leave it as soon as you can. The three ways of engaging the mind provide a good blueprint for doing this.

LET BE

Be mindful of when you are starting to feel pressured, uneasy, exasperated, frustrated, stressed, or upset. Be with the experience and explore its different parts. Label them to yourself: *tense . . . worried . . . annoyed . . . sad.* This will increase activity in the prefrontal cortex (the part of the brain behind your forehead), which will help with top-down self-control. Naming to yourself what you are experiencing will also decrease activity in the amygdala—which functions like an alarm bell in the brain—and help you calm down.

Explore what might be vulnerable and soft deeper down, such as sad feelings of being left out in high school beneath a flare of anger at not being included in a meeting at work. Simply be with what is flowing through awareness without rehashing it or working up a righteous case about it. Step back from red zone reactions and observe them, like stepping out of a movie and moving twenty rows back in the theater to watch it.

LET GO

Shift into letting go. Understand that Reactive thoughts and feelings are generally not good for you—and others as well. Decide whether you want to hold on to these thoughts and feelings or release them.

Exhale slowly, and relax your body. Let feelings flow. As appropriate, cry, yell, grumble with a sympathetic friend, or simply sense that anxiety, irritation, and hurt are draining out of you. Be skeptical of the assumptions, expectations, or beliefs that made you worried, stressed, frustrated, or angry. Consider the meanings you gave to situations or how you interpreted the intentions of others, and let go of whatever is untrue, needlessly alarmist, or mean-spirited. Be mindful of the sense of leaving the Reactive mode.

LET IN

Start letting in whatever helps you feel that your needs are being met. Tune into a sense of determination and capability inside. Give yourself some pleasure: wash your hands in warm water, eat an apple, or listen to music. Pleasure releases natural opioids that soothe and settle the brain's stress machinery. Think of things you feel grateful for or glad about, things that bring a little smile. Connect with someone you like, either directly or in your imagination. Let yourself feel cared about; also recognize your own warm heart. Identify thoughts or perspectives that are accurate, useful, and wise. Be mindful of the sense of entering the Responsive mode.

Build Up Responsive Resources

Most people experience the Responsive mode many times a day, but usually blow right by it before it has a chance to sink in. So look for opportunities to feel like your needs are being met. For example, while inhaling, notice that there is plenty of air to breathe. At least in this moment, you are safe enough—moment after moment after moment. As you finish one task or another—an email sent, a child's hair brushed, a car's gas tank filled up—stay with the sense of satisfaction. When someone smiles at you or you remember a person you love, keep feeling connected. Be mindful of green zone experiences, value them, and stay with them. Let them into yourself, taking half a dozen seconds or longer to help them begin hardwiring their way into your brain.

In this way, you'll be developing inside yourself the underlying fullness and balance that are the basis of the Responsive mode. You'll also be gradually reducing the sense of deficit and disturbance that triggers the Reactive mode. Internalizing green zone experiences builds up a core of inner strengths. In a positive cycle, this fosters more experiences of the Responsive mode and therefore more opportunities to grow inner resources. Then you can handle larger and larger challenges, staying green inside even when the world is flashing red, with a bone-deep resilient well-being that nothing can penetrate and overwhelm.

When faced with a challenge, be mindful of which particular need—for safety, satisfaction, or connection—is at stake. Deliberately call upon your inner strengths related to meeting these specific needs, and I'll be showing you many ways to do this in the pages ahead. Then, as you experience mental resources, you can reinforce them in your nervous system.

I've sailed some, and I've managed to capsize a boat that didn't have a keel. If the mind is like a sailboat, growing inner resources is like strengthening and lengthening its keel. Then you can live more boldly, trusting that you can explore and enjoy the deeper waters of life, and handle any storms that come your way.

KEY POINTS

- Your brain is shaped by your experiences, which are shaped by what you attend to. With mindfulness, you can rest your attention on experiences of psychological resources such as compassion and gratitude, and hardwire them into your nervous system.

- There are three major ways to relate to and engage the mind usefully: be with it, decrease what is painful and harmful, and increase what is enjoyable and beneficial.

- We have three basic needs—safety, satisfaction, and connection—that we manage by avoiding harms, approaching rewards, and attaching to others. These needs and the ways we meet them are loosely related, respectively, to the reptilian brain stem, mammalian subcortex, and primate/human neocortex.

- Well-being comes from meeting our needs, not denying them. When we experience that our needs are sufficiently met, the body and mind enter the "green zone" Responsive mode, and there is a sense of peace, contentment, and love. When needs feel unmet, we're disturbed into the fight-flight-freeze "red zone" Reactive mode, and there is a sense of fear, frustration, and hurt.

- The Responsive mode is our home base, but we're easily driven from home and prone to getting stuck in the red zone due to the brain's negativity bias, which makes it like Velcro for bad experiences but Teflon for good ones.

- To stay in the green zone, take in experiences of your needs being met, which will grow inner resources. Then you can handle larger and larger challenges with resilient well-being.

CHAPTER 3

LEARNING

Think not lightly of good, saying, "It will not come to me." Drop by drop is the water pot filled. Likewise, the wise one, gathering it little by little, fills oneself with good.

—The Dhammapada

Going on a long hike, we need to bring food and other supplies. Similarly, on the road of life, we need psychological supplies such as compassion and courage. How do we get these supplies *into* the neural "backpack"?

THE GROWTH CURVE

We do it by *learning*. This is a broad term that goes far beyond memorizing multiplication tables. Any lasting change of mood, outlook, or behavior requires learning. From childhood onward, we learn good habits, character strengths, and skillful ways to interact with others. Healing, recovery, and development are forms of learning as well. About a third of our attributes are innate in our DNA, while the other two-thirds are acquired through learning. This is very good news, since it means we have great influence over who we become, who we learn to be. Suppose you would like to be calmer, wiser, happier, and more resilient. Having read many comic books as a kid, I think of these inner strengths as sort of like superpowers.

Learning is the superpower of superpowers, the one that grows the rest of them. If you want to steepen your growth curve in life, it pays to learn about learning.

How Learning Happens

Any kind of learning involves a change in neural structure or function. These changes occur in two stages, which I call *activation* and *installation*. In the first stage, activation, there is an experience, such as feeling liked. All experiences—all thoughts, sensations, daydreams, worries, and anything else passing through awareness—are based on underlying neural processes. A particular experience is a particular state of mental/neural activity. Then in the second stage, installation, this experience is gradually consolidated in long-term storage in the brain. Over time, passing states become installed as lasting traits. (I'm using the term "trait" broadly.)

There's a saying in brain science based on the work of Donald Hebb: "Neurons that fire together wire together." The more they fire together, the more they wire together. In essence, you develop psychological resources by having sustained and repeated experiences of them that are turned into durable changes in your brain. You become more grateful, confident, or determined by repeatedly installing experiences of gratitude, confidence, or determination. Similarly, you center yourself increasingly in the Responsive, green zone—with an underlying sense of peace, contentment, and love—by having and internalizing many experiences of safety, satisfaction, and connection.

The Essence of Self-Reliance

This is the fundamental "how-to" of healing, training, and personal growth. You can apply it to developing interpersonal skills, motivation, peace of mind, or anything else you want inside yourself. It's the essence of self-reliance. Even the most fulfilling situations, occupations, and relationships may change. Sooner or later, one way or another, the bottom could fall out. But whatever you have inside yourself is with you always. Just like you can't unlearn how to ride a bicycle, you won't unlearn the inner strengths you grow over time. And the harder your life is and the less support you're getting from external sources, the more important it is to look for those little opportunities each day to highlight a useful or enjoyable experience and consciously take it into yourself.

Unfortunately, this process of deliberately internalizing beneficial experiences is rarely taught explicitly. In schools, workplaces, and trainings, people are instructed in various things—but they're not usually taught *how* to learn. When you *learn how to learn*, you gain the strength that builds the other strengths of resilient well-being.

HEAL Yourself

You can guide the structure-building processes of your brain in four steps, which I summarize with the acronym HEAL:

ACTIVATION

1. **H**ave a beneficial experience: Notice it or create it.

INSTALLATION

2. **E**nrich it: Stay with it, feeling it fully.

3. **A**bsorb it: Receive it into yourself.

4. **L**ink it (optional): Use it to soothe and replace painful, harmful psychological material.

The first step of HEAL is the activation phase of learning. You start with a useful or enjoyable experience of some kind. The rest of HEAL is the installation phase, in which you begin the process of turning that beneficial experience into a lasting change in your brain. The fourth step, Link, involves being aware of positive and negative material at the same time. It is optional for two reasons: the first three steps alone are sufficient for learning, and sometimes people are not yet ready to engage their negative material.

In the rest of this chapter, we'll explore the HEAL steps in detail, including how to have beneficial experiences more often and then help them have enduring value. I'll show you how to identify and grow the strengths you need most. And you'll see how to use the Link step to ease and even end difficult, upsetting, or limiting thoughts, feelings, and behaviors, including from childhood.

ENCOURAGE BENEFICIAL EXPERIENCES

Ask yourself what stands out in a typical day. The car that cut you off, the dish that broke, and the frustrating project at work? Or the pleasure of eating breakfast, the sense of determination as you push through a difficult task, and the beauty of a sunset? Think about your relationships. What draws your attention when you're interacting with others: the many things going well, or the one word that stings?

If you're like most people, it's the negative that stands out. Because of the brain's negativity bias, painful and harmful experiences move to the front of awareness, while enjoyable and useful ones fade into the background. This may have short-term benefits in harsh conditions, but over time it causes much wear and tear on your body and mind. In effect, the brain is tilted toward survival but against long-term health and well-being. By tilting back toward positive experiences, you just level the playing field. This is not about wearing rose-colored glasses or looking on the bright side. It's hardheaded pragmatism based on recognizing that life is often difficult, you need mental resources for it, and you can build these inner strengths by guiding your brain's learning process.

This process starts with *experiencing* the good you want to grow inside yourself. There are two ways to have a beneficial experience. First, you can simply *notice* and focus on one that you are already having. Second, you can deliberately *create* an experience, such as calling up a feeling of self-compassion or sitting down to meditate. Let's explore each of these.

See the Jewels Around You

Nearly everyone has many positive experiences each day, most of them mild and brief. For example, it feels good to drink water if you're thirsty or put on a sweater if you're chilled. It's hard to get through a day without feeling friendly toward at least one person. Do you take notice of these experiences and highlight them in your awareness? Or do you pass by them and just move on to the next thing?

Each day is like a path strewn with many little jewels: the small ordinary beneficial experiences of life. It's easy to overlook these and step right over them. But then we get to the end of the day and ask, "Why don't I feel richer inside? Why does it feel like I'm running on empty?"

The jewels are already there. Why not pick some of them up? If an experience feels good, it usually *is* good for you and often for others, too. Don't dismiss enjoyable experiences as lightweight and trivial, and don't think that grinding, wearying, stressful experiences are somehow the foundation of a good life. It's the opposite: positive experiences fill us up, while negative ones wear us down. Sure, some pleasures are bad for a person over time, such as eating too many sweets. And some psychological resources are grown in part through unpleasant experiences. For example, you can strengthen your moral compass through appropriate guilt and remorse. But on the whole, if something feels good, that's usually a sign it's a jewel worth reaching for.

Our experiences are built from five elements, and each element is a type of jewel you can weave into the fabric of your brain and your life. These elements are *thoughts* (e.g., beliefs, images), *perceptions* (e.g., sensations, sounds), *emotions* (feelings, moods), *desires* (e.g., values, intentions), and *actions* (the sense of posture, facial expressions, movement, or behavior). For example, in an experience of gratitude, there could be a thought of something a friend gave you, a perception of relaxing, an emotion of gladness, a desire to express appreciation, and an action of writing a thank-you note.

While you are having a beneficial experience, other things could be in awareness as well. Your back might be aching as you enjoy stroking the fur of a cat in your lap. These other things do not cancel out the beneficial experience. Both are true: the negative and the positive, the bitter and the sweet. You can let the bad be while also letting in the good.

This is not positive thinking. It's *realistic* thinking: seeing the whole mosaic of the world around you and the complexity of your experience, despite the brain's tendencies to fixate on a handful of bad tiles in that mosaic while overlooking the jewel-like good ones.

Create Some Jewels Yourself

Noticing enjoyable or useful thoughts, perceptions, emotions, desires, or actions that are already occurring is the primary way to have a beneficial experience. The experience is here, and it's authentic and real. Why not gain something from it?

Additionally, you could *create* beneficial experiences, such as getting some exercise or thinking about someone who likes you. There are several ways to create these kinds of experiences.

First, *look for* good facts. These are the things that support your well-being and welfare—and often that of others. You can find them in many places, including your current situation, recent events, ongoing conditions, the past, and the lives of others. You can also find good facts inside yourself; consider your talents, skills, and good intentions. You can even find them in hard times, such as seeing the kindness of others as you go through a loss. Second, *produce* good facts by taking action. For example, you could do something as simple as shifting in a chair to feel more comfortable. Or you could make something good happen in a relationship, such as by listening carefully to someone.

Facts are facts, and you can count on them. You're not making anything up. Once you've found a good fact, turn the recognition of it into an embodied experience. Know that the fact is really true; give yourself a sense of conviction about it and trust in it. Be aware of your sensations as you recognize the fact, with a sense of softening and opening in your body. Tune into your feelings and allow the experience to be emotionally rich. For an extended experience of this, try the practice in the box on the next page.

Third, directly *evoke* a positive experience, such as relaxing at will, calling up a sense of determination, or letting go of a resentment. Because of experience-dependent neuroplasticity, repeatedly having and internalizing a particular experience in the past makes it easier and easier to evoke it in the present. It's like being able to push a button on your inner jukebox and quickly get the song of a useful experience playing in your mind, since you've recorded it again and again.

Whether you're noticing an experience or creating one, each day is full of opportunities to have beneficial thoughts and emotions, perceptions and desires. Just knowing that this is true is itself a good experience!

CREATING A BENEFICIAL EXPERIENCE

This practice focuses on gladness, but you can apply the methods in it to any experience you'd like to create for yourself.

Think of something—a fact—that you are glad about. It could be small or large, in the present or in the past. It could be a thing, an event, an ongoing condition, or a relationship. It could be a spiritual being or the entire universe.

Be aware of your body and open to gladness . . . gratitude . . . comfort . . . happiness. There could be an easing of tension, a letting go of stress or disappointment.

Explore different elements of the experience. Be aware of thoughts such as "I'm fortunate" . . . perceptions, especially body sensations . . . emotions like delight or quiet joy . . . desires, perhaps to give thanks . . . and actions such as a soft smile.

Think of other things that you are glad about. Help the knowledge of them to become a rich experience by using the suggestions just above.

HELP EXPERIENCES HAVE LASTING VALUE

When you have a good song playing in your mind, turn on the recorder and take it into your brain. Otherwise, it will have little if any long-term value.

Sometimes there's incidental learning from passing thoughts and feelings. But most of the beneficial experiences that people have in the course of a day make no difference. There is no shift in outlook, no change of heart, no acquisition of inner resources.

Much the same happens in psychotherapy, coaching, and human resources programs. As a longtime therapist, it's humbling and haunting to know that most of the hard-won experiences that clients had in my office did not lead to any real change for the better. This was my fault, not theirs. I think that professionals are generally effective at *activating* various states of mind but generally poor at *installing* these as beneficial traits in the brain. Consequently, the greatest opportunity is not in pursuing even better ways for our clients, patients, or students to have useful experiences. It is in getting better at converting the experiences they're already having into durable changes in neural structure and function.

Whether you are doing this for yourself or helping someone else, the essence of installation is simple: *enrich* the experience and *absorb* it. In your mind, enriching an experience means keeping it going and feeling it fully, while absorbing it feels like receiving it into yourself. In your brain, enriching is a matter of heightening a particular pattern of mental/neural activity, while absorbing involves priming, sensitizing, and increasing the efficiency of the brain's memory-making machinery.

This may seem abstract at first, but it's a natural, intuitive process, and we all know how to do it. Everybody has had experiences they've slowed down for and received into themselves. In practice, this process is usually pretty quick, lasting a breath or two, and the enriching and absorbing aspects of it sort of mush together. But when you are learning anything new—including how to learn itself—it's useful to unpack the pieces and focus on each one individually. Then in the flow of your day, they'll fit back together again as you take in the good as often as you like.

Enriching an Experience

There are five ways to enrich an experience:

1. **Lengthen it.** Stay with it for five, ten, or more seconds. The longer that neurons fire together, the more they tend to wire together. Protect the experience from distractions, focus on it, and come back to it if your mind wanders.

2. **Intensify it.** Open to it and let it be big in your mind. Turn up the "volume" as it were by breathing more fully or getting a little excited.

3. **Expand it.** Notice other elements of the experience. For example, if you're having a useful thought, look for related sensations or emotions.

4. **Freshen it.** The brain is a novelty detector, designed to learn from what's new or unexpected. So look for what's interesting or different about an experience. Imagine that you are having it for the very first time.

5. **Value it.** We learn from what is personally relevant. Be aware of why the experience is important to you, why it matters, and how it could help you.

Any one of these methods will increase the impact of an experience, and the more the better. But you don't have to use all of them every time. Often you'll simply stay with something for a little while and feel it in your body, and then move on to the next experience.

Absorbing an Experience

You can increase the absorption of an experience in three ways:

1. **Intend to receive it.** Consciously choose to take in the experience.

2. **Sense it sinking into you.** You could imagine that the experience is like a warm soothing balm or a jewel being placed in the treasure chest of your heart. Give over to it, allowing it to become a part of you.

3. **Reward yourself.** Tune into whatever is pleasurable, reassuring, helpful, or hopeful about the experience. Doing this will tend to increase the activity of two neurotransmitter systems—dopamine and norepinephrine—that will flag the experience as a "keeper" for long-term storage.

The first three steps of HEAL—have a beneficial experience, enrich it, absorb it—are the essence of learning. To use the metaphor of a fire, these steps are like finding or lighting it, protecting and fueling it, and taking its warmth into yourself. You can use them on the fly multiple times a day, ten seconds here and half a minute there. You could also set aside a few minutes or more to focus on a particular experience, such as by doing the practice in the box.

This is not about holding on to experiences. The stream of consciousness is constantly changing, so trying to cling to anything in it is both doomed and painful. But you *can* gently encourage whatever is beneficial to arise and stick around and sink in—even as you are letting go of it. Happiness is like a beautiful wild animal watching from the edge of a forest. If you try to grab it, it will run away. But if you sit by your campfire and add some sticks to it, happiness will come to you, and stay.

ENRICHING AND ABSORBING A SENSE OF CARING

Bring to mind someone you naturally care about, such as a friend, child, partner, or pet. Help yourself have a sense of warmth, liking, appreciation, compassion, or love.

Once you are having an experience of caring, start to enrich it. Lengthen it by disengaging from distractions and coming back to it if your mind wanders; keep it going breath after breath. Open to this experience, letting it fill you, becoming more intense. Expand it by exploring different aspects of caring: thoughts . . . sensations . . . emotions . . . desires . . . actions (such as putting a hand on your heart). Bring an attitude of curiosity to help the experience stay fresh and vivid. Consider how the sense of caring could be important for you, relevant, and valuable.

Then focus on absorbing it. Consciously intend to receive this experience into yourself. Sense these warm feelings spreading inside, becoming a part of you. Look for what feels good about being caring: how it is enjoyable, heart-opening, and rewarding. Sink into caring as it sinks into you.

GROW THE STRENGTHS
YOU NEED MOST

My parents were loving, worked long hours, and did the best they could. Still, for multiple reasons, including my own withdrawal, I did not experience a lot of empathy from them. Children need a rich "soup" of empathy from their parents, but for me it was a thin broth. Also, I was younger than my classmates due to a late birthday and skipping a grade, and this plus my nerdy temperament led to many experiences of being ignored or rejected at school. My needs for safety and satisfaction were handled well enough. But my need for connection was not. Lots of little things add up over time, and when I left home for college, it felt like there was a big hole in my heart—an empty, aching place inside.

I didn't know what to do about it. I tried being cautious and determined, which helped me feel safe, but did nothing to fill the hole. I had fun in college and got good grades—addressing the need for satisfaction—but this, too, left me hollow inside. It was as if I had scurvy—an unmet need for connection—and required vitamin C, but I was taking vitamin A and vitamin B. These were fine in their own right, but not the key nutrient I was missing.

Then, midway through my freshman year, everything changed when I began to notice, feel, and take in *social supplies*—such as a group waving me over to eat with them or someone being friendly on the way to class. This was what I needed; *this* was my vitamin C. Bit by bit, day by day, many little experiences gradually filled that hole in my heart.

So, what's your vitamin C?

Find Your Key Resources

The three basic needs offer a useful framework for identifying your most important inner resources. When you know what these are, you can usually find opportunities each day for experiencing and growing them.

CLARIFY THE CHALLENGE

As a doctor might ask, where does it hurt?

You may be dealing with an external challenge such as interpersonal conflict, a stressful job, or a health problem. Or you could be facing an internal challenge such as harsh self-criticism or feeling unwanted. Sometimes there's a one-two punch. For example, tension with someone might be stirring up self-criticism inside you.

Pick a challenge, and then consider the needs at stake in it, in terms of safety, satisfaction, and connection. More than one need could be involved, but often there's one that stands out. Pain, threat, or immobilization—often with feelings of anxiety, anger, or powerlessness—are clues that *safety* is at risk. Blocks to reaching your goals, failure, loss of property, or a life with little pleasure—perhaps with a sense of disappointment, frustration, or boredom—suggest that *satisfaction* needs tending. Interpersonal conflict, rejection, loss, or devaluation—often with feelings of loneliness, hurt, resentment, envy, inadequacy, or shame—flag the need for *connection*. If you tend to push aside a particular need—such as connection, for instance, by blaming yourself when people mistreat you—that's the one to be extra sure you're not overlooking.

IDENTIFY THE RESOURCES THAT COULD HELP

A particular need is best met by inner strengths that are *matched* to it. If your car is running on fumes, gasoline is the solution, not a spare tire. These are major mental resources for the basic needs, and we'll explore each one of them in these pages:

- **Safety:** being on your own side, determination, grit, sense of agency, feeling protected, clarity about threats, feeling all right right now, calm, relaxation, peace

- **Satisfaction:** gratitude, gladness, pleasure, accomplishment, clarity about goals, enthusiasm, passion, motivation, aspiration, feeling of enough-ness already, contentment

- **Connection:** compassion for others and oneself, empathy, kindness, self-worth, skillful assertiveness, forgiveness, generosity, love

If you're chilled and need to warm up, just about any type of jacket will work. In the same way, any of the resources above will usually help with the need to which it is related. Additionally, a challenge is often best approached with a combination of inner strengths. This said, closely matching a specific resource to a specific challenge can be very useful. For example, I was small going through school and often picked last for sports teams. Those old feelings of embarrassment and weakness have been particularly healed by many experiences of capability and toughness high up in the mountains.

As you consider a major challenge and the need(s) at the heart of it, see if any of the resources listed above stand out. Ask yourself:

- What, if it were more present in my mind these days, would really help?

- What inner strengths could help me stay in the Responsive mode when I'm dealing with this challenge?

- If this challenge began in the past, what would have been really helpful to have experienced back then?

- Deep down, what experience do I still very much long for?

The answers to these questions point to a key resource, your vitamin C. Also remember this: Love is the multivitamin, the universal medicine. Love helps us feel safe, whether as a scared child getting a hug or as an adult walking with a friend through a dark parking lot. Love is deeply satisfying. And love draws us immediately into a sense of connection. If it's hard to identify a key resource for a challenge, no worries. In one form or another, try love.

Internalize Key Resources

Once you've identified a key inner strength, use the HEAL steps to have experiences of it that you install in your nervous system.

There might already be a sense of this resource in the back of your mind, and then all you have to do is *notice* it and bring it to the foreground of awareness. Suppose that you're insecure about your performance at work, and you've realized it would help to feel more respected by your colleagues. It's possible that they're actually saying or doing little things that show they recognize and appreciate you, and there is a fleeting sense of this passing through your awareness. If this is happening, you could try to be more mindful of this experience.

You could also *create* experiences of an important inner resource. For example, if you wanted to feel more respected by your coworkers, you could deliberately look for facts that demonstrated this, such as a sense of camaraderie, a tone of approval, or being asked your opinion. You could also take action, such as speaking up and letting yourself shine more in meetings. When you do find facts that are natural opportunities to experience an inner strength, slow down to focus on them and help the recognition of them become a beneficial experience.

Once you're having an experience of the resource, shift into the installation phase of learning. To repeat, you can enrich the experience by staying with it, letting it fill your mind, opening to it in your body, exploring what could be fresh or new about it, and recognizing what is relevant or important about it. Also absorb it into yourself by intending that it become part of you, sensing it sinking in, and finding what is enjoyable about it.

Focus on Experiences, Not Conditions

Any chance to feel and to grow a key mental resource is a valuable opportunity. Know what experiences you are looking for, and when you find them, really take them in.

It's natural to think about your resources in terms of people, events, or settings outside of you. But then imagine what these conditions would help you feel inside yourself. It's important to care about external conditions in their own right, including for their effects on others, but for our own practical purposes, they're largely means to the ends of the *experiences* we value. For example, suppose that a person would like to have a romantic partner. Why might someone seek this "condition"? At least in part, because then there could be experiences of love, self-worth, joy, and other good things. Certainly we should try to improve the conditions of life for ourselves and others. But these are often slow to change, if at all. On the other hand, when the focus shifts from means to *ends*, from conditions to experiences, so many possibilities open up. For example, even without having a romantic partner, a person could find other ways to experience some kinds of love, self-worth, and joy.

I'm not trying to minimize the value of a romantic partner or any other external condition. But if that condition is out of reach, there could still be ways to experience some aspects of it. And in terms of internalizing resources into the brain, *experiences are independent of the conditions that evoke them.* Once a song is playing on the inner iPod, it can be "recorded" regardless of what its source was. Among other things, this means you can help yourself to have and internalize parts of key experiences that may have been missing when you were young, even though the conditions of childhood are long behind you.

This distinction between conditions and experiences, between means and ends, is very important, and losing sight of it is the cause of much stress and unhappiness. For example, a person could get fixated and driven about attaining a particular condition such as a new car or a promotion, and then lose sight of the needs that attaining the condition would fulfill, and miss opportunities to experience those needs being met in other ways. Is the car *itself* important, or is a sense of comfort and safety what's most valuable? Is the promotion itself the crux of the matter, or is it a sense of success and satisfaction? To put it a little differently, people are not unhappy because they don't have a car or a promotion. They're unhappy because they don't feel comfortable, safe, successful, and satisfied.

When you know the true ends, the experiences that matter most, then you can look for when they are already occurring, or deliberately create them. You may not be able to have every bit of an important experience, such as feeling loved by a wholly nurturing parent as a child or cherished by a romantic partner today. But you can almost always find aspects of it that you can internalize—such as feeling liked by a friend or appreciated by a co-worker. You may not be able to heal a wound entirely or fill up every bit of the hole in your heart. Still, something is better than nothing. And the somethings you take in may eventually help you get the everything you long for.

USE FLOWERS TO PULL WEEDS

When I started taking in the good in college, sometimes I'd be aware of two things at once, such as feeling appreciated in the front of awareness with a sense of worthlessness off to the side. When this happened, it would feel like the positive material was touching and going into the negative material, gradually filling up empty places inside and soothing old wounds.

This is the essence of the Link step in the HEAL process. It may sound exotic, but there are many ordinary examples. You could be worried about something, and talking with a friend is reassuring.

Perhaps there's a setback at work, and you remind yourself of times when you were successful. Maybe an acquaintance is snippy and it hurts, and then your loving grandfather comes to mind and that's comforting. When you use the first of the three major ways to relate to your mind to simply *be with* something that's upsetting, this naturally links a disturbing experience with the always inherently undisturbed field of awareness.

Using the Neuropsychology of Learning

Linking is a powerful method. The brain learns through association, and when two things are held in awareness at the same time, they affect each other. The key is to make sure that what's beneficial stays more prominent than what's painful or harmful. Then the positive will purify the negative, rather than the negative contaminating the positive.

Because of the negativity bias, stressful experiences over the course of your life have been prioritized for storage in your brain, especially into what's called *implicit memory*: the residues of lived experience that shape your expectations, ways of relating to others, and background sense of what it feels like to be you. The remnants of the past affect you in the present, and you can use Linking to reduce and even replace them. When negative material is reactivated from memory stores, it becomes unstable and open to positive material that's also present in awareness. Then the negative material goes through a neural process of *reconsolidation* that can incorporate those positive influences. In the garden of the mind, the first three steps of HEAL plant flowers. In the fourth step, you use flowers to pull weeds.

Being Skillful with Linking

To do Linking, a person must be able to hold two things in awareness, keep the positive material more prominent, and not get hijacked by the negative. Practicing mindfulness will increase your capacity to do these things. If you get pulled into the negative, drop it and focus only on the positive. Later on, you can allow the negative to come back alongside the positive in awareness. Most experiences of Linking are fairly brief, under half a minute, but you can take longer if you like.

Look for positive material that is naturally matched to the negative material, such as the key resources related to particular challenges that we explored in the previous section. For example, experiences of calm are a soothing antidote to anxiety or nervousness; being included these days helps heal being left out in the past. If the negative material feels young, focus on nonverbal, tactile, gentle, and sweet aspects of the positive material, much as you would offer to a child of that age.

There are two ways to enter into Linking. You'll often start with something positive, such as the sense of a key resource. While having that experience, you can then bring to mind some negative material for which it would be good medicine. The other way is to start with something that is uncomfortable, stressful, or harmful, such as a lot of anxiety before giving a presentation of some kind. In the sequence of *let be, let go, let in*, after letting your feelings be as long as you like and then letting go of them, you would find positive material to replace what you had released, such as a sense of calm from knowing that people are actually interested in what you have to say. So far you've used just the first three steps of HEAL. Then if you want, you could move into the fourth step and bring the positive material into contact with remnants or layers of the negative material in order to uproot it most fully.

Be cautious with negative material. If it's too powerful, you can grow mental resources for addressing it through the first three HEAL steps alone. Then when you feel ready, you can link it to positive material in three increasingly intense ways.

KNOW IT

The least intense and generally safest way to engage negative material is to be aware of just the *idea* of it, such as the knowledge that you lost a parent when you were a child. Keep the idea "over there," off to the side in your mind, while a rich, enjoyable positive experience is "right here" under the spotlight on the stage of awareness.

FEEL IT

Next, if you feel comfortable doing so, you could have a *felt sense* of the negative, such as some loss and mourning from losing a parent. Remember to keep this material smaller, dimmer, and less active than what's positive in awareness. If the negative starts to draw you in, refocus on the positive.

GO INTO IT

Last, you could imagine or sense that the positive is *contacting and penetrating* the negative material. This is the most intense way to engage it; consequently, it may be the most effective, but it is also the riskiest. So be careful and pull attention away from the negative if it's too much for you. There could be an image of the positive experience sinking into hollows inside and gradually filling them up, or easing bruised, wounded places like a soothing balm. A useful perspective could replace limiting or painful beliefs. More adult parts of you could hold, comfort, reassure, and cherish younger parts. Compassion could touch suffering.

When you do Linking, be resourceful and creative. Stay on your own side, helping whatever is beneficial to prevail in your mind. Use your imagination and go with your intuition. For example, one time when I was doing Linking, an image came to me of waves of love lapping on the shore of my mind, with a rising tide.

A Process of Linking

Here is an extended experiential process that you can use to address painful or harmful thoughts, sensations, emotions, or desires: what I am calling the negative material. Going into this process, know what the positive material is—the beneficial experiences, the inner strength(s), the vitamin C—that you'd like to associate with the negative material. Remember to drop the negative if it becomes too big or overwhelming, stay on your own side, and adapt this practice to your needs. It will probably take at least a few minutes, and you can spend as much time with it as you like.

1. **Have.** Call up a sense of being on your own side. Then begin creating an experience of the positive material. You could remember when you really experienced it, perhaps a time you felt particularly safe, satisfied, or connected. Or imagine being in the kind of setting or relationship that would naturally evoke this resource experience. Or access this experience directly, dropping into the sense memory of it in your body. Or use any other way that works for you to have a clear experience of this positive material.

2. **Enrich.** Stay with the positive material. If your mind wanders, come back to it. Help it to become more intense, filling

your awareness. Explore this experience, sensing it in your body, opening to its emotional aspects. Recognize how it is relevant, important, and valuable for you.

3. **Absorb.** Intend and sense that this experience is sinking into you, sifting down into you, becoming a part of you. Receive it into yourself, like a gentle warmth spreading inside. Recognize what feels good about it, what seems wholesome and enjoyable.

4. **Link.** When you're ready, be aware of the idea of the negative material off to the side and the positive material large and rich in the foreground of your awareness. It's fine if your attention moves quickly back and forth between the positive and the negative, but generally see if you can be aware of them both at the same time. Stay with the idea of the negative alongside the positive experience for a few breaths or longer. Then, as long as it's not overwhelming, you could have more of a felt sense of the negative—but still off to the side, smaller and less powerful than the positive. Again, explore what this is like for a few breaths or more, resting in the positive, taking refuge in a strong sense of the positive, while there is also a feeling of the negative in the background of awareness.

Finally, if it seems right, imagine that the positive is touching and going into the negative. Perhaps like waves spreading out into sore or empty places inside . . . or reassurance and comfort and kindness soothing sad and hurt parts of you . . . or the light of insight spreading into shadows . . . or adult compassion and love holding and perhaps murmuring softly to young hurting parts. There could be a sense of the positive being received into the negative, slipping into it and under it, perhaps gently dislodging it, releasing it from your mind. Try not to intellectualize about the negative or get into a big story about it; keep this as experiential as possible. If the negative becomes too big or you get lost in it, drop it and focus on only the positive material. Once you are reestablished in the positive, you can become aware of the negative again if you like.

Finishing up, let go of anything negative and rest in the positive material. Enjoy it. You've earned it.

KEY POINTS

- We acquire mental resources through *learning*. This happens in two stages: activation and installation. First, there must be an experience of the resource or related factors, and second, that experience must be converted into a lasting change of neural structure and function.

- Without installation, there is no learning, healing, or development. Getting better at installation will steepen your growth curve, and these skills can be applied to anything you would like to develop inside yourself.

- This is not about positive thinking. It is about realistic thinking, seeing the whole mosaic of reality with its problems and pains as well as its many, many reassuring, pleasurable, and useful parts.

- You can grow inner strengths in four steps, summarized as HEAL: have a positive (enjoyable, beneficial) experience, enrich it, absorb it, and (optionally) link it to negative material.

- You can use the HEAL steps to grow the mental resources that would help you the most these days. Use the framework of the three basic needs—safety, satisfaction, and connection—to identify the inner strengths that are matched to your challenges.

- The Link step is a powerful way to use positive psychological material to soothe, reduce, and even replace negative material.

- We can learn how to learn. Learning is the inner strength that grows all the other ones.

PART TWO

RESOURCING

CHAPTER 4

GRIT

*Toughness is in the soul and spirit, not
in muscles.*

—Alex Karras

Grit is dogged, tough resourcefulness. It's what remains after all else
has been ground down—and when even grit is worn away, people
are in big trouble.

I learned some scary lessons about this when I went camping one
winter with my friend Bob. We spent the day slogging through deep
snow in the backcountry near Sequoia National Park, climbing uphill in our snowshoes. Through previous experiences in wilderness
and other intense settings, we had both developed a fair amount of
gritty endurance and felt confident that we'd be all right. Bob has
tremendous natural vitality, and he powered ahead to break the trail
for us. As it grew dark and we needed to make camp, we were both
exhausted, and Bob began shivering uncontrollably. He had poured
out so much energy without refueling himself that he was sliding
into hypothermia, the first stage of freezing to death. In effect, he
had used up his internal supply of grit, which put his need for safety
at mortal risk. The temperature was dropping rapidly, and I was
extremely drained myself. We hurried to set up the tent, get into
our sleeping bags, light the stove, drink hot water, and eat hot food.

Soon Bob's teeth stopped chattering and after a while we began to feel normal again. After a long cold night, we broke camp in the morning and made our way slowly back to civilization, this time much more careful about not using up everything inside ourselves.

This was a dramatic lesson in the importance of developing grit in the first place for the challenges you know about and the ones waiting around the corner to surprise you. If Bob and I had not acquired deep reserves through our experiences and training, something very serious could have happened. Second, it was a sobering reminder of the importance of refueling grit along the way, and not letting the needle hit "empty."

Grit is based on several things. To increase and refuel the grit inside you, we'll start by exploring *agency*, the sense that you can make things happen rather than being helpless. Then I'll cover different aspects of determination, including patience and a fierce tenacity. We'll finish with ways to increase your vitality, including through accepting and appreciating your body. For additional perspectives on grit, I recommend Angela Duckworth's book with this title, and her related research.

AGENCY

Agency is the sense of being a *cause* rather than an effect. Agency is present if you deliberately pick a blue sweater over a red one or listen to someone express an opinion and think, "Nah, I don't agree with that." With agency, you are active rather than passive, taking initiative and directing your life rather than being swept along. Agency is central to grit, since without it a person can't mobilize other internal resources for coping. If you've been knocked down by life, agency is the first thing you draw on to get up off the floor.

Unlearning Helplessness

Agency is the opposite of helplessness. Research by Martin Seligman and others has shown that we are very susceptible to acquiring *learned helplessness* through experiences of powerlessness, immobilization, and defeat. Consider a child who can't escape bullying or an adult who's been assaulted. Or situations in which there is a mismatch between responsibility and resources, such as one person in a downsized corporation trying to do the jobs of three people. Even subtle forms of powerlessness wear people down over time, such as repeatedly trying to get the sustained empathic attention of a partner and finally giving up. A growing sense of pessimism, futility, and hopelessness drags down mood, coping, and ambition, and is a major risk factor for depression.

It typically takes many experiences of agency to compensate for a single experience of helplessness, another example of the brain's negativity bias. To prevent helplessness in the first place or to gradually unlearn it, look for experiences in which you are making a choice or influencing an outcome. Then focus on and take into yourself the sense of being an active agent: a hammer rather than a nail. In particular, look for experiences in which there is a vigorous sense of making something happen or pushing something forward. It could be deciding to go for one last repetition of lifting a weight at the gym or holding a yoga pose ten seconds longer. In an interaction, you could decide you've had enough and it's time to exit. In a meeting, if your idea has been misunderstood and brushed aside, you could stick your hand up and make your point again.

In life, there are times when we step back and take a hard look at something—such as a relationship, living situation, or way of parenting—and in a deep and honest way recognize that we need to make a significant change. It could be hard, it could be painful, but we choose the change. This also is agency.

When Agency Is Limited

When your options are very limited, look for the little things you *can* do, and focus on the feeling of agency regarding them. For example, if you're facing a health crisis, could you decide to go online to learn more about it? In an argument with a family member, can you feel like *you* are deciding what to say—and what not to say? The more powerful the forces bearing down on a person, the more important it is to find ways to experience some sense, any sense, of agency.

If we can't exercise agency "out there," with words or deeds, we can usually make choices "in here," inside the mind. Unless something is extraordinarily painful, physically or emotionally, we have the power to shift attention away from it to something more enjoyable or useful. For example, when I sit in my dentist's chair, I'll deliberately remember walking through high alpine meadows in Yosemite National Park. We also have power over how we think about situations and relationships, such as putting them in perspective. The less power we have "out there," the more important it is to exercise agency "in here." When you make deliberate choices inside your mind, try to recognize that fact and register the feeling of being the chooser.

Many things happen *to* a person. Still, we can experience a sense of agency in how we *respond* to them. If this is possible in even the most terrible, most horrific situations of all, then it is possible in everyday life. Consider this passage from Viktor Frankl, after surviving the Holocaust:

We who lived in concentration camps can remember the men who walked through the huts comforting others, giving away their last piece of bread. They may have been few in number, but they offer sufficient proof that everything can be taken from a man but one thing: the last of the human freedoms—to choose one's attitude in any given set of circumstances, to choose one's own way.

Tend to the Causes

It makes sense to focus on where we do have agency instead of where we do not. For example, there's an old apple tree in our back-yard that I've pruned and watered over the years—but I've never been able to *make* it give me an apple. In much the same way, there are so many things in life for which all we can do is tend to the causes, but we cannot force the results. We can nurture and guide our children—but we can't control what they end up doing as adults. We can be decent and loving toward other people—but we can't make them love us. We can eat nourishing food, exercise, and go to the doctor—but we may get sick anyway. All we can do is water the fruit tree.

We may not be able to directly create something we want, but we can still encourage the underlying processes that will bring it into being. Knowing this brings a sense of both responsibility and peace. In terms of responsibility, it's on each of us to tend to the causes that we can influence, to use the agency that we do have. Take some time to consider major areas of your life, such as health and relationships, and look for simple realistic things you could do that would cause them to improve. For example, it might make a real difference to have a solid breakfast, stand up from your desk at least once an hour, and get to sleep at a reasonable time most nights. Slowing down and just listening to a friend can help a relationship. Seemingly little things often cause big results. As you consider your life in this way, if you see something that calls for more tending, let that seeing become a feeling of commitment that you enrich and absorb, giving over to it so it moves you to action. At the end of each day, know deep down that you did the best you could.

Meanwhile, enjoy a greater sense of peace. Many of us go through life insisting, metaphorically speaking, that seeds give us apples. But then we lock onto particular results, and get frustrated and self-critical if they don't happen. The truth is, ten thousand causes upstream of this moment are bringing it into being, and most of them are beyond anyone's control. Recognizing this fact and accepting it may feel initially alarming, like being swept along down a river. But as you get used to it, you could feel an easing of tension and drivenness, and a growing serenity.

DETERMINATION

Challenging things happen to every person, and *determination* is the steadfast fortitude we draw on to endure, cope with, and survive them. A person can be wounded, frail—and very determined. In fact, some of the most determined people I've known were the most burdened, such as a young Haitian friend working his way out of terrible poverty, and another friend who is dealing with gradually losing his vision. Determination might sound grim, but in fact it can be playful and lighthearted. Consider this description I once heard of Thich Nhat Hanh, the peace advocate, monk, and Buddhist teacher: "A cloud, a butterfly, and a bulldozer."

Determination has four aspects to it: *resolve, patience, persistence,* and *fierceness*. As you go through your day, you can use the HEAL steps to turn experiences of these aspects into an even stronger sense of determination inside yourself.

Resolve

Resolve is aimed toward a goal. Otherwise it's like having a car with a big engine but no destination. To get an embodied sense of what resolve feels like, think about times when you've been serious about a goal. What's the look on your face when you are absolutely committed to something? When you mean business? There could be a gravity about you, a quality of steely intent. When you have an experience of resolve, stay with it for a dozen seconds or longer to help yourself become even more resolute and determined.

Of course, we need to be adaptable in pursuit of our goals. I can get too finicky about little details and lose sight of the end in my fixation on means. True resolve is like sailing a boat, tacking back and forth into the wind, zigging and zagging to get to your destination.

Along the way, have heart. Otherwise, resolve can become cold and top-down—like a harsh inner boss yelling at you—rather than warm and bottom-up. Resolve includes passion, fieriness, and even joy. Think of something you "should" do but don't stick with, and take some time to imagine doing it in a more wholehearted way. As you imagine this, notice that your sense of commitment naturally increases. Let this greater sense of resolve sink in.

Patience

One time as a teenager I had one of those haunting experiences that sticks with you. Looking down from our apartment late at night, I saw a workman trudging steadily along the sidewalk. I didn't know if he was headed home or about to start another shift. Either way, he looked tired. Maybe his feet hurt, maybe he wished he had a different life. But he kept on going. He made me think of my parents and other people who kept on doing the right thing, fulfilling their obligations, patiently putting one foot in front of the other.

Many of the mistakes in my life have come from being impatient: annoyed with how long something was taking, pressuring others to hurry up, or jumping to a conclusion. Patience doesn't mean ignoring real problems, but life is full of delays and discomfort, and sometimes we just have to wait.

Patience might sound like a modest virtue, but it's the essence of two primary factors in mental health and worldly success. The first is *delay of gratification*, the willingness to put off immediate rewards for the sake of a greater future reward. The second is *distress tolerance*, the capacity to endure a painful experience without making a bad thing worse, such as "self-medicating" with overeating or alcohol.

Pick some part of your life that's frustrating or exasperating, and see if you can imagine being more patient about it. What would it feel like to be more patient? There could be a sense of accepting things as they are, bearing your stress or pain, one breath after another, one step after another. What, inside yourself, could help you be more patient? You could focus on the feeling that you are still alive, still basically OK, even when you're not getting what you want. You could deliberately let go of irritation, and you could remember that whatever you're putting up with is likely a brief period in the larger span of your life. If you were more patient, what would be some of the good results? You would probably feel better and be more effective, and others might be happier with you. When you experience patience, use the Absorb step in HEAL to receive it into yourself, with a sense of actually becoming more patient. Try the Link step to hold both patience and frustration in your awareness, and to use patience to ease and calm any tense or irritated places inside.

Persistence

Different versions of this fable appear in many cultures: Once upon a time, some frogs fell into a bucket full of cream. The sides were steep, none of the frogs could escape, and one by one they gave up and drowned. But one frog kept swimming, working its little legs methodically to stay afloat. And slowly, ever so slowly, it churned the cream into solid butter. Then the frog hopped out of the bucket and lived happily ever after.

I love this fable and the idea that, no matter what, you can still persist on your own behalf, if only inside your mind. Even if your efforts don't pay off, you'll know in your heart that you tried, and that in itself feels honorable and comforting.

It's usually the small, undramatic, sustained efforts over time that make the most difference. Imagine that you want to push a large boat at a dock out into the water. You could run full speed and smash into the boat, but that would be painful and have little effect. Or you could stand on the end of the dock, lean against the boat—and keep on leaning.

Is there something important in your life that would be good to keep leaning into? Perhaps regular exercise, meditation, or gradually mending a relationship with a spouse or a teenager, one brief positive interaction at a time. You can accomplish big things by persisting with small actions. Suppose you've thought about writing a book, but it seems overwhelming. Well, could you write two pages over the course of a day? Do this every few days, a hundred times spread out over a year, and you've got a book.

Sometimes the most important things to persist with are your thoughts and feelings. I've known people who pushed bravely ahead through tough external conditions, such as hazardous jobs, but gave up when it was important to be emotionally vulnerable. Here, too, small steps move a person forward. Try staying with a scary feeling one breath longer than usual or being a bit more revealed to another person. Notice the results. Most likely nothing bad will happen, and in fact it will feel good and others will be fine. Then register and internalize the sense of taking a small risk and it turning out well. Build on this to take the next step, and on and on.

Fierceness

Determination taps into something ancient and wild inside each one of us. I had a startling experience of this when I was nineteen, helping to take a group of schoolchildren on a backpacking trip through the Yosemite high country.

It was late spring, and the nights were still very cold. We made a lunch stop in a large jumbled boulder field near a river, then kept going. A mile or so later, one of the kids realized he'd left his jacket back where we'd stopped. I said I'd go get it and then meet up at the campsite for dinner. I set down my pack, hiked back to the boulder field, searched through it, and found the jacket. But I couldn't relocate the trail. I cast about in all directions, surrounded by rocks, trees, and broken ground. The nearest person could have been miles away. I was lost, wearing just a T-shirt, no water, no food, and night coming on. I started to panic.

Then a strange feeling came over me, that I would do whatever it took to survive. There was a feral intensity, not cruel or evil, but like a hungry hawk swooping down upon a rabbit: not mean or vengeful but fiercely committed to its own life. The intensity burned away the panic, and it energized me to search carefully for the faint traces of the trail. I eventually found it and, many miles later, rejoined my friends late that night.

The sense of that fierce will to endure has stayed with me, and I've drawn on it many times. Paradoxically, just knowing that I can go there if need be has helped me turn the other cheek in certain situations, in effect using something feral to stay civilized. We *are* animals, strong and tenacious enough to rise to the top of the food chain. In some approaches to psychology, religion, and child rearing, you'll find an underlying idea that the primal basement in everyone's mind is full of smelly, nasty creatures that must be locked away. Sure, we need to regulate ourselves. But we don't need to fear and shame the wild things inside.

Think of a good experience you've had of being fierce and strong, perhaps while standing up for someone, moving through wilderness, or handling an emergency. Imagine what it would feel like and how it might help to bring some of that determined intensity into a challenging situation today. Looking back, I see that I've often been too tame, too buttoned up. Perhaps you, like me, could benefit from opening a door inside and drawing on something that's fiercely helpful.

VITALITY

What we think and feel is grounded in physical sensations and movements. For example, psychologists have found that the cognitive development of children is shaped by sensorimotor activity, and that the perspectives and moods of adults are highly influenced by pleasure and pain, energy and fatigue, and health and illness. In similar ways, we're affected by how we feel about our bodies and treat them. I've spent years thinking that my body was too skinny, too fat, too this, too that, while working it hard, like spurring a horse uphill day after day. If a person doesn't like his or her body, it's harder to take good care of it; then vitality declines, and with it, grit and resilience. We need to accept, appreciate, and nurture the body, and treat it more like a friend than a disposable beast.

Accepting Your Body

How do you feel about your body? Many people are self-critical, embarrassed, or ashamed about their bodies. One reason for this is that we are bombarded with countless messages from early childhood onward about how girls and boys, women and men, and people in general are supposed to look. Think about what you have heard and seen over the years from your parents, classmates, and friends, and from advertising and media.

Few can actually meet these standards—but we internalize them anyway, looking in the mirror and judging and pressuring and shaming ourselves. Then it's all too easy to obsess about food or exercise, go through yo-yo dieting, and perhaps even develop an eating disorder.

To have more acceptance of your body, start by bringing to mind some people you like and respect. How much does the way they look matter to you? Probably very little. Also think about meeting new people. How long does it take to get past how they look to a deeper sense of them? Probably less than a minute. We worry about what others are thinking about how we look, but usually they are thinking about it about as much as we are thinking about their appearance . . . not much at all!

What does it feel like to know that how you look is not important to most people? What does it feel like to know that in fact how you look is just fine to them? Take some time with this, and help this knowing establish itself in you. If your attention is drawn to that one put-down about your weight, pull it back to what you know about how most people see you. Help a sense of conviction develop, the feeling that you truly believe that others accept how you look. Perhaps say to yourself things like: "Others are busy and have their own concerns . . . they are not spending time criticizing my appearance . . . even if one person is judgmental, others are accepting . . .

they feel fine about me." Open to related feelings of relief and reassurance. Relax and let the good news sink into you.

Then take the next step, and see if you can be as accepting of your body as others are. It's fine to have realistic goals about fitness and health. Meanwhile, your body is what it is, and you can accept it. Pick a part of your body that you like, such as your fingers or eyes. Accept this part of your body, and take in the sense of accepting it.

Then, starting with your feet, systematically try to accept each major part of your body. You can look at yourself directly, use a mirror, or bring to mind different parts. Do what helps you move into acceptance. If you can't accept a part of your body, move on to other parts. Say to yourself things like: "Left foot, I accept you . . . right foot, you are acceptable to me . . . left lower leg, I can accept you as you are . . . right lower leg, accepting you, too." Let the sense of acceptance grow and spread in your mind. Relax and let go of judgments. You could use the Link step to use that acceptance to calm and ease any self-criticism about your body.

Appreciating Your Body

Besides accepting your body, can you appreciate it? Suppose you had a friend with a body like yours—as well as the talents, skills, good heart, and other virtues that you have. Also suppose that this friend is preoccupied, self-conscious, or self-critical about his or her body in whatever ways you are yourself. Imagine some of the reasonable, compassionate, and encouraging things you might say to this friend. You could write these down if you want. Then say them to yourself inside your mind or even out loud. Also try the practice in the box.

BODY, THANK YOU

As with any practice, adapt this to your needs, take good care of yourself, and disengage from anything that is too uncomfortable. Take a few breaths, relax, and get a sense of being on your own side. Bring to mind others who appreciate, like, or love you, and open yourself to feeling cared about.

Imagine your life as a kind of movie, starting when you were very young and moving forward to the present. Watching this movie, see some of the ways that your body has protected and served you. Even if it has had limitations, disabilities, or illnesses, it has still taken care of you in so many ways. Imagine your body saying how it has helped you, such as: "I grew eyes so you could see . . . I built a marvelous brain so you could think and dream . . . my arms and hands have let you hold those you love . . . I've enabled you to walk and work, dance and sing, and enjoy so much pleasure."

Scan the major parts of your body from feet to head. See if you can appreciate each one of them, perhaps saying to yourself things like: "Feet, thank you for carrying me along . . . Thighs, you've done your job countless times and I'm very grateful . . . Heart and lungs, all those beats and breaths, oh my goodness I so appreciate you . . . Hands and hips, I accept you as you are . . . Chest and arms, neck and shoulders, head and hair, thank you for everything you've done for me."

Imagine your body in the days to come. See yourself in different situations over the next year—perhaps with friends, at work, or at family gatherings—and imagine that you completely accept your body in them . . . imagine that you really appreciate your body in them . . . imagine that you enjoy your body in these situations. Be aware of how good it would feel to relate to your body in these ways. Let these good feelings sink into you as you sink into them.

Nurturing Your Body

Physical health is a tremendous aid to resilience, and the most consequential threats to safety are threats to the body. As a psychologist, I'm not offering medical advice, but the commonsense basics are obvious:

- Have a balanced and nourishing diet.

- Get a good night's sleep.

- Exercise regularly.

- Minimize or eliminate intoxicants.

- Act early to assess and treat potential health problems.

Most people know what they should do. The key is drawing on agency and determination to do it. Consider the list just above and see if there are any actions that you think you should take. If there's something you know you should do but you're not doing it, pause and think about the consequences: for what you feel like on a typical day . . . for other people . . . for yourself in a year or ten or twenty . . . for how long and how well you want to live.

People commonly put off improving their personal health practices. It's so easy to say, "I'll start tomorrow." But the tomorrows keep adding up, and the years go by. Then something comes along—an injury, a serious illness, or a major stressor—that lands hard on a weakened constitution, like a tree branch falling on a house hollowed out by termites. It's motivating, not morbid, to realize that we're all running out of runway, that it's time to change something that could add quality years to your life.

Imagine how good it will feel to make that change. Take a little time to imagine the sense of health and energy in your body . . . the feelings of self-respect . . . the appreciation of others . . . the hopeful years ahead with friends and family. If doubts come up about whether you'll stick with the change, simply bring your attention back to a rich experience of the rewards of doing it. Use one or more of the five aspects of the Enrich step in HEAL to strengthen the experience: stay with it, help it be more intense, open to it in your body, find something new or fresh about it, and recognize how it is personally valuable to you. All this will tend to be motivating, inclining your brain toward this new behavior.

Then, of course, make the change. Look for simple, practical ways to support yourself. For example, if you want to cut down on the carbohydrates you eat, have a salad with some protein for lunch and don't bring home a box of donuts. If you want to get more sleep, turn off the TV by ten o'clock. If you need more exercise, set up a regular walk with a friend. If alcohol is tempting, keep it out of your house. And when you do take action, even in small ways, pause for a moment and really feel the rewards of doing so.

I don't mean to trivialize how hard it can be to adopt a new health habit. I've had my own struggles for sure. But your odds of success go up dramatically when you "tend to the causes" in three ways: recognize the need for a change, take appropriate actions, and internalize experiences of the rewards that come to you. Keep watering the tree, and most likely it will bear you good fruit.

KEY POINTS

- Just a few experiences of being trapped, powerless, and defeated can lead to "learned helplessness," which undermines coping and ambition, and is a risk factor for depression. So it's important to look for what you *can* do, if only inside your mind, especially in challenging situations or relationships.

- In so much of life, you can tend to the causes, but you can't control the results. Knowing this fosters both responsibility and inner peace.

- Use the HEAL steps to internalize experiences of resolve, patience, and persistence.

- Mental health is sometimes framed as suppressing our primal, animal nature. But then parts of the self that are wild and wonderful get locked away. Being able to tap into a fierce, feral intensity makes a person more resilient.

- How you feel about and treat your body affects your health and vitality, and these in turn affect your thoughts, feelings, and actions.

- Just as you probably don't care much about what others look like, most if not all people are not critical of your body. Accept your body for what it is, and focus on what you appreciate about it.

- Don't put off sensible actions for your physical health. It's always easy to start tomorrow. Instead, ask yourself, "What can I do today?"

CHAPTER 5

GRATITUDE

*Piglet noticed that even though he
had a Very Small Heart, it could hold
a rather large amount of Gratitude.*

—A. A. Milne

Gratitude and other positive emotions have many important benefits. They support physical health by strengthening the immune system and protecting the cardiovascular system. They help us recover from loss and trauma. They widen the perceptual field and help us see the big picture and the opportunities in it; they encourage ambition. And they connect people together.

We tend to spend our lives seeking to feel good in the future, but this is stressful and tiring in the present. With gratitude, you feel good *already*—so let's explore how to develop it and other positive emotions by giving thanks, taking pleasure, feeling successful, and being happy for others.

GIVING THANKS

Recall a recent time you gave thanks, out loud or just inside your mind. Perhaps while eating a meal, when getting a hug, or looking up at the sky. There's a natural feeling in the body when we're thankful, a sense of easing, a need met, satisfaction.

Think about some of what you've been given, such as friendship and love, an education, life itself, and a universe that bubbled into being more than 13 billion years ago. And that's just for starters. Alongside whatever is painful or difficult in a person's life, there is always already so much to be thankful for.

As a little experiment, bring to mind something that you have been given, and then think or say "thank you" for it. Thankfulness feels good in its own right. Additionally, Robert Emmons and other researchers have found that it brings a remarkable collection of benefits:

- More optimism, happiness, and self-worth; less envy, anxiety, and depression

- More compassion, generosity, and forgiveness; stronger relationships; less loneliness

- Better sleep

- Greater resilience

Ways to Grow Thankfulness

Thankfulness is not about minimizing or denying hassles, illness, loss, or injustice. It is simply about appreciating what is *also* true: such as flowers and sunlight, paper clips and fresh water, the kindness of others, easy access to knowledge and wisdom, and light at the flick of a switch.

Be mindful of any reluctance to see these gifts, such as a concern that this will make you lose track of problems or lower your guard. It helps to remember that you can be deeply thankful while maintaining a sharp-eyed clarity about what could go wrong.

When there is pain in life, see if there are any gifts that come along with it. For example, our kids have grown up and left home and we miss them dearly, but there's also great appreciation for their blossoming as adults.

One of the key findings of the research on gratitude is the striking value of celebrating the gifts of life with others. I remember sitting with my wife and a hundred other parents at an event at our daughter's preschool, watching the kids perform little skits and then sing together. It was so sweet and we felt so grateful for our children and their teachers.

Try to make thankfulness a regular part of your day. For instance, you could put a reminder to give thanks beside your desk or on your car's dashboard. You could keep a journal of things you're thankful for, or write a letter to someone saying what you appreciate about that person. One powerful method is to reflect on three blessings in your life before falling asleep. Help the recognition of what you've received become feelings of appreciation, reassurance, and even awe and joy. Use the HEAL steps to take these feelings into yourself, sinking into them as they sink into you. The practice in the box will give you an extended experience of this.

BEING THANKFUL

Take a breath and relax. Think of someone you really appreciate. What are some of the things that this person has given to you? Let these memories become feelings of thankfulness, and let those feelings sink in.

Think about what has been fortunate in your life, such as your natural talents ... when or where you were born ... who your parents were ... good luck that has come to you. Without taking away from your own efforts, open to feeling thankful for your good fortune.

Consider the world of nature: flowers ... trees ... flocks of birds ... all the life in the ocean. In your mind or out loud, see what happens when you say "thank you." Let your thanks fill your heart and ripple outward.

Consider some of the many objects you use in a day that have been made by or invented by other people, often long ago: wheels ... safety pins and smartphones ... soy sauce.... streetlights and stop signs ... zippers and belt buckles. Handed to you, gifted to you ... deserving of your thanks.

Step back and think about all the things that have happened to bring our Milky Way galaxy into being ... our solar system ... our own sweet planet ... life emerging over 3 billion years ago ... our own human species appearing ... your grandparents being born ... and having children ... who met and had you. So many things coming together to bring you into being. Looking upstream at the river of time, you can see so many things to be thankful for. Wow. Thank you.

TAKING PLEASURE

Our pleasures include lovely sights, fascinating ideas, and good times with others. Healthy pleasures crowd out unhealthy ones; after eating an apple, there's less interest in a candy bar. If you're having a stressful or upsetting experience, simple pleasures such as listening to music can move the needle of your internal stress-o-meter out of the red zone and back toward green. And if you use the HEAL steps to repeatedly internalize experiences of pleasure, over time you will feel increasingly pleased from the inside out. This will help to reduce desires for pleasure from the outside in.

Unfortunately, many people do not experience much pleasure. Some of the reasons for this are general. As Søren Kierkegaard wrote, "Many of us pursue pleasure with such breathless haste that we hurry past it." In fast-paced cultures, it takes a deliberate effort to slow down and relish a pleasure. Other reasons are more individual, and see if any of these apply to you. A person might believe something like: "My role is to make sure that others are enjoying themselves, not me." Or think: "How dare I enjoy this when so many people are suffering?" Or there could be inhibitions against feeling certain pleasures, perhaps because they are associated with shame.

If you do find a block to pleasure inside yourself, you can move past it by using the three ways to engage your mind:

- **Let be:** Explore the block with mindfulness and self-compassion; be curious about how it developed.

- **Let go:** Relax any tension in your body related to the block; challenge beliefs associated with it (e.g., find reasons why they're wrong); consciously decide that you don't want the block to control you.

- **Let in:** Say to yourself ideas that contradict the beliefs associated with the block (e.g., "I deserve pleasure, too"); imagine how good it would feel to let yourself have more pleasure.

It might seem that there is just no pleasure to be had in a pain-filled life. But if you can accept the fact of the pain—drawing on mindfulness, self-compassion, and other inner resources to help you bear it—that will make more room for pleasure. Your attention will not be so caught up in resistance to pain, and you will be free to recognize and enjoy everything else.

Taking pleasure is itself an expression of agency. Even in the worst of times, there are opportunities for simple pleasures: a sip of water in a parched mouth, the call of a bird, a memory of kindness, a blade of green grass reaching up through a crack in a dirty sidewalk. I'll never forget visiting a large residential facility for people who were severely developmentally disabled. As I rounded a corner, I saw a young man lying on a cot in the hallway, unable to walk and with an estimated IQ of about 20, and he gave me an incredibly radiant smile, quivering with delight at the pleasure of a human face.

A Pleasure Diary

The harder the life, the more important it is to experience and internalize psychological resources—including the sense of pleasure. A sweet way to do this is to keep a pleasure diary on paper or simply in your mind.

Consider some of the many sensory pleasures you might encounter today. Sights of skyscrapers, faces, stones. Sounds of music, water, laughter. Tastes of fruit, tea, cheese. Touches of soft cloth, a child's hand, a pillow. Smells of orange, cinnamon, rose, curry. The pleasures in movement, stretching, walking, running.

Also consider mental or emotional pleasures, such as finishing a crossword puzzle or learning an interesting fact. Meditation or prayer can be deeply enjoyable. So can playing music or cooking something new for dinner. It feels good to accept yourself, and to let go of thoughts and feelings that have been painful.

And of course there are social pleasures. Laughing together, cooing over a baby, accomplishing something as a team, understanding another person better—all so good. Some of the deepest pleasures are moral: a feeling of integrity, knowing that you have done the right thing when it was hard to do.

As you go through your day, deliberately flag opportunities for pleasure. On a piece of paper, you could keep count of the pleasures you receive—and probably be happily surprised at the total by nighttime. Or simply take a few minutes before sleep to look back over the day and remember some of its many pleasures.

FEELING SUCCESSFUL

There is an architecture of aims inside us that ranges from microscopic regulatory processes within individual cells all the way up to our loftiest aspirations. Living is inherently goal-directed. Experiences of meeting your goals feel good, lower stress, and build positive motivation. They reassure you that you're making progress, which helps you stay in the Responsive mode—in the green zone—as you go through your day. There are *outcome* goals such as getting out of bed in the morning, coming to a good understanding with someone at work, and washing the dishes after dinner. And there are *process* goals—ongoing values and aims—such as being honest, learning and growing, and taking care of your health.

If you think about it, you can see that you are accomplishing many outcome and process goals every hour. For example, as you walk across a room, each step is a goal. This may sound trivial, but for a toddler learning to walk, each step is a victory. In a conversation, each word understood and facial expression deciphered is a goal attained. At work, every email read, text sent, and point made in a meeting is an accomplishment.

Since each day is full of goals, large and small, it is full of opportunities to take in experiences of successful goal attainment. Doing this builds up an internal sense of *being* successful, which helps us weather criticism and be less dependent upon the approval of others. Much self-importance and acting superior is a compensation for underlying feelings of failure and inadequacy. Consequently, feeling like a success deep down can help people lighten up and take themselves less seriously. A durable sense of being successful comes from internalizing many experiences of small successes, not from seeing a big trophy outside such as a fancy car parked in the driveway.

Feelings of Failure

We all accomplish countless outcome and process goals each day. Yet many people do not feel very successful. One reason is the negativity bias. Internal alarms go off when we don't meet goals, and dopamine activity drops in the brain, which feels bad and heightens anxiety, tension, and drivenness. But when we do meet our goals, we often don't recognize it. People can be inattentive or numb as they do one task after another, or so focused on whatever is around the bend that they zoom through the finish line as they rush on to the next race.

When you do notice an accomplishment, how often do you feel the success, if just for a moment? It's common to block feelings of success due to fears of being ridiculed or punished for standing out or thinking you're somebody special. And when you do have a sense of success, do you slow down to take it in and hardwire it into your nervous system? The number of actual failures in any person's life is tiny compared to the vast number of goals that have been successfully attained. But the failures are highlighted by the brain, associated with painful feelings, and stored deeply in memory. This crowds out a legitimate and well-earned sense of being an accomplished and successful person.

The fear of failure is worsened if you grew up with a lot of criticism, even if there was also a lot of love. It's also worsened if you are part of a company—or, more broadly, an economy—that's incentivized to keep people on the proverbial hamster wheel, with real success always slightly out of reach. Make your first dollar? It's on to the first thousand. Make your $1,000? Well, so-and-so made $10,000. Get promoted? Stay hungry. Win a championship? Better repeat next year. Work harder, stay later, give 110 percent . . . but it's never quite enough. The goalposts keep getting pushed back.

Feeling afraid of being a loser can be motivating, whether for a child or for a CEO. But over the long haul, those negative feelings wear people down and lower performance. Feeling reasonably successful *already* helps people aim high, recover from setbacks, and achieve their best.

Since you actually *are* moving from success to success hundreds of times each day, it's simple justice to *feel* successful.

Everyday Success

Consequently, try to notice some of the many goals you accomplish daily. Be mindful of *succeeding at small outcomes*, such as preparing a meal, adding paper to a printer, or reading to a child. Producing even a single small result—let's say eating a spoonful of soup—usually involves many smaller accomplishments, such as holding the spoon, dipping it into the bowl, bringing it to the lips without spilling, getting the soup into the mouth, and returning the spoon to the table. Any one of these little accomplishments is a chance to feel successful.

Notice *progress toward big outcomes*, such as raising children to be independent adults, completing classes for a degree, or saving money for retirement. Each step may be short, but as the hours and months and years add up, it feels good to realize that you are covering a great distance.

Recognize that you are *continuing to fulfill ongoing process goals*. Consider how you've stayed in integrity and functioned appropriately at home and at work. Also think about some of the disasters that you've already avoided today: no bad fall in the bathroom, no fire in your home. Really, this is a kind of success, and it's worth appreciating.

Even in a very difficult life, it's possible to feel successful in many ways. The more that you feel defeated about some things, the more important it is to recognize your victories in many other things. When you have an experience of success, open to it and take it in, using the HEAL steps. And try the practice in the box for a rich and embodied sense of this.

FEELING SUCCESSFUL

Take a few breaths and relax. Get a sense of being on your own side. Bring to mind some small outcome goals you've already accomplished today, such as getting out of bed, drinking water, and doing tasks at home or work. Help yourself feel successful at accomplishing these. Open to related feelings of pleasure, reassurance, and worth. Enrich these experiences by sustaining them . . . feeling them in your body . . . recognizing what could be personally important about them. Absorb these experiences by sensing them sinking into you, becoming a part of you . . . focusing on what is enjoyable about them.

Recognize progress toward big outcomes such as planting a garden, getting to know a new friend, or preparing for a promotion at work. Let this recognition become an experience of success, and take this into yourself.

Be aware of fulfilling ongoing process goals such as still breathing, still going on living . . . being warmhearted and fair-minded . . . making efforts . . . enjoying life. Open to a sense of success and related feelings such as contentment.

As you experience a sense of success, you can use the Link step to connect it with "negative material" such as disappointments, worries, tension and drivenness, or feeling inadequate. Keep the sense of success prominent in the forefront of awareness, and drop the negative material if it grabs you. Imagine the positive making contact with the negative, sifting down into frustrated places inside, perhaps reaching down into experiences of failure when you were younger. Let the sense of success calm, soothe,

and bring perspective to the negative material. As you finish, let
go of anything negative and simply focus on the sense of success.

BEING HAPPY FOR OTHERS

Think of a time when you saw a child laughing, heard a friend share
some good news, or learned that a co-worker had recovered from a
serious illness. This is the feeling of being happy for others, sometimes called *altruistic joy*, and it's grounded in our long history as
social beings. Living together in small bands, our hunter-gatherer
ancestors flourished when those they lived with flourished as well.
Consequently, there was evolutionary pressure to develop both
compassion for the suffering of others and happiness for their good
fortune. Sometimes we do compete for finite, scarce resources, such
as applying for a job. But if things are reasonably fair, we can be
good sports and respect the success of others. And most aspects of
life are truly win-win: one person's good health, stable marriage,
and thriving children do not stop another person from also having
these things.

That Happiness Which Is Always Available

To paraphrase the Dalai Lama: *If you can be happy when others are
happy, you can always be happy, since there is always someone somewhere
who is happy.* It's easiest to feel delighted or glad for family members,
friends, and others who've treated you well, but it's also possible to
feel happy for challenging acquaintances and even strangers. You
can feel happy for individuals and groups, those close to home or far
away, pets, and in fact any living thing.

Just as there are many kinds of others, there are many kinds of
good fortune. You could be glad about recent events in someone's

life or pleased about ongoing conditions such as health, prosperity, and a loving family. If you know a child, just think about how much he or she is learning each day. Perhaps things are getting better for someone you care about. Just the simple fact that people are alive is reason enough to be happy for them.

Think of a time when someone was really glad for you—perhaps you'd been promoted or a health scare had turned out to be nothing—and see if you can remember how that touched you. Turn it around: the support, recognition, and good wishes that were given to you are exactly what you give to others when you are happy for them.

Doing this benefits you even as it benefits others. Altruistic joy feels good, opens the heart, and brings a sense of positive connection to a wider world. Other people sense it when you're happy for them, which strengthens and deepens relationships.

An Antidote to Disappointment and Envy

Walking down a busy city street, it's easy to forget that the natural social environment for a human being is a band of about fifty people. This is how we lived for most of our time as a species, and how our tool-manufacturing hominid ancestors lived for more than 2 million years before that. Consequently, we've evolved a brain and a mind that are designed for a very specific setting: fairly small groups.

Whether that group is a Stone Age tribe, an eighth-grade class, or co-workers in an office, it's been important to know where one stands in comparison to others. So we measure ourselves against both friends and rivals. We feel reassured and worthy when it looks like we're doing better than they are. But we tend to feel bad when it looks like we're not. With social media, we compare the entire movie of our lives—whose warts we know painfully well—to the carefully edited highlight reels of everybody else, and it's easy to feel disappointed, diminished, and envious.

Happiness for others is a natural antidote to these feelings. It can pull you out of self-critical or bitter preoccupations and shift your mood in a positive direction. But thinking about the good fortune of other people may lead to painful comparisons that block gladness for them. To get through this block, begin by recognizing the blessings that *you* have received, the joys you have found, the things you have achieved, and the contributions you have made to others. Whatever is good in your life remains good even if another person has something great. Also know that fortunate people suffer too. Like everyone, they face disease, death, and inevitable loss. Remember that whatever is happening in anyone's life is a local ripple in a vast river of causes. Most of those causes are impersonal, such as the luck of the DNA draw or the social class of parents. This means you don't need to take their "ups" or your "downs" so personally.

Start with people who are easy to be happy for. When you feel glad for their good fortune, slow down and take it in. Then try this with other people. Do this repeatedly, and you'll develop the habit of being happy for others—a large-hearted way to find a reliable happiness.

KEY POINTS

- We seek to feel good in the future, but this is often stressful in the present. Poignantly, the pursuit of happiness can push it out of reach. With gratitude, we feel good already.

- Giving thanks for what is beneficial does not prevent us from seeing what is harmful. In fact, the ways that thankfulness supports physical and mental health make us more resilient and more able to deal with challenges.

- Pleasure is easy to dismiss, but it is a rapid way to lower stress or to disengage from an upset. Wholesome pleasures crowd out unwholesome ones. The more you feel already full of pleasure, the less you'll strain for it outside yourself.

- Because of the negativity bias, we notice when we fail to reach a goal while missing the fact that meanwhile we're succeeding at hundreds of other goals. Look for opportunities to feel successful many times each day. Take in these experiences and use them to compensate for and heal feelings of failure or inadequacy.

- If you can be happy about the happiness of others, you can find a lasting happiness.

CHAPTER 6

CONFIDENCE

*Too many people overvalue what they
are not and undervalue what they are.*

—Malcolm Forbes

Two friends of mine had a baby girl when I began writing this book, and now she's a toddler and eagerly walking about. Her parents make sure she doesn't get hurt, and they give her just enough help to get whatever she's trying to touch or taste. If she bonks herself and cries, they're sympathetic and soothing. Before her first birthday, she experienced thousands of brief interactions in which her parents were helpful and encouraging, and in which she felt capable and happy. The essence of these experiences has been woven into her nervous system, building up resources to meet her need for connection.

For all of us, this process of learning continues through childhood and into adulthood. Besides parents, it involves siblings and peers, teachers and bosses, friends and enemies. If it goes reasonably well, we acquire a sense of being cared about, worth, and self-assurance that helps us cope with challenges, especially in relationships. We develop *confidence* in ourselves, in others, and in the world. But if there's been too much disapproval and rejection, and too little encouragement and support, then a person tends to lack confidence and be insecure, self-critical, brittle, and less resilient.

To grow the inner strength of confidence, we'll start by grounding this topic in the evolution of the social brain and the effects of secure and insecure attachment. Then I'll cover how to feel more secure in the core of your being and stay on an even keel of emotional balance. We'll finish by exploring how to stand up to the inner critic and strengthen your sense of self-worth.

THE SOCIAL BRAIN

Our relationships and their effects are the result of the long slow evolution of the *social brain*, beginning with the emergence of mammals. Unlike most reptiles and fish, mammals raise their young, frequently bond with a mate—sometimes for life—and live cooperatively in many ways with others of their kind. To manage the complexities of social life, mammals required more information processing power, and thus more powerful brains. In proportion to the size of their bodies, mammals usually have bigger brains than reptiles and fish. And only mammals have the six-layered *neocortex*, the thin and convoluted sheet of tissue that is the outer "skin" of the brain and the neural basis of complex experiences, communications, and reasoning.

Their social capabilities have enabled mammals to thrive in an extraordinary range of environments—seals in Antarctic waters, mice in blistering hot deserts, bats in pitch-dark caves—and propelled one mammal in particular to become the dominant species on the planet. In an evolutionary spiral, the survival benefits of relationships for our primate and human ancestors encouraged the development of a more "social" brain, which enabled even more complex relationships, which called for an even more capable brain. For example, the more social the primate species—the larger the grooming group, the more complex the alliances and rivalries—the larger the cortex. Since our hominid ancestors began using tools to make more tools about 2.5 million years ago, the brain has tripled in volume. Much of this build-out is devoted to socially relevant capabilities such as empathy, language, cooperative planning, compassion, and moral reasoning.

As the brain grew larger, childhood grew longer. A newborn chimpanzee's brain is half the size of an adult's—but a human baby's brain is just a quarter of the size it will eventually become. Hominid and early human brains needed more time to mature into their full size, which extended the dependency of children on their mothers. A hominid or early human mother tending to a child was less able to gather food, run from a predator, or defend herself. She had to rely on others, including her mate, her kin, and her band. This drove the evolution of human pair bonding, the investment of fathers in child rearing, and the development of the whole village that it takes to raise a child.

Being dependent may sound like a weakness, but it is one of our greatest strengths. Spreading to the farthest corners of the globe, even walking upon the moon, humans have become so wildly successful through *depending* on each other: children on their parents, one parent on another, families on communities, and communities on the many adults who aren't raising children.

The root of the word "confident" means "to have trust or faith." If others are dependable, we develop trust in them as well as faith in our own worth. But if others are not dependable, it's normal to develop a sense of inadequacy, self-doubt, even shame. This is particularly true in childhood, when we are both most dependent on others and most affected by our negative experiences.

SECURE AND INSECURE ATTACHMENT

Physically, our lives depend upon getting enough air, water, and food. Additionally, we must get *social supplies*—especially when we're young and need lots of empathy, skillful caregiving, and love. It is our biological nature to need to feel cared about. In fact, we need to feel that we're *worth* being cared about. For some children and teenagers, these needs are well met. But for others, not so well. The needs of a young person land on parents, siblings, and classmates who have their own needs and issues. With a variety of people, every child naturally, implicitly, asks again and again: "Do you see me?" "Do you care about me?" "Will you treat me well?" The psyche is built from the bottom up, from the residues of countless experiences, and the foundational layers were laid down in the first years of your life.

By a child's second birthday, the accumulating effects of many experiences with caregivers usually coalesce into a fundamental *attachment style*. Through grade school and high school, interactions are shaped by the original attachment style and tend to reinforce it. Unless there has been a major shift—such as through significant personal growth—this style continues to operate deep inside important adult relationships, especially if they are intimate.

To simplify a large body of research, when parents and other caregivers are usually attuned, responsive, loving, and skillful—reliably delivering a "good enough" stream of social supplies—children are likely to become *securely attached*. They have a feeling of being loved and worthy, as well as strong capacities to soothe and regulate themselves. People with such an internalized secure base are able to explore the world, tolerate separations, and recover from hurt and disappointment. They're comfortable saying how they feel and what they want, since they've had many experiences in which this went reasonably well. They don't cling to other people or push them away. Deep down, they have a core sense of connection needs met, and their Attaching system is centered in the Responsive mode. They are confident.

On the other hand, when children experience their caregivers as frequently unavailable, insensitive, cold, rejecting, punishing, or abusive, then they are likely to become *insecurely attached*. (There are three types of insecure attachment—avoidant, ambivalent, and disorganized—and my summary here won't explore the distinctions among them.) People with this attachment style tend to feel inadequate and unworthy, and unsure if they truly matter to others. Given their personal history, they have doubts about others being reliably attentive, supportive, and trustworthy. Consequently, they tend either to keep their distance and not expect much or to cling to other people. Having taken in relatively little caring from others, they're less able to be compassionate toward themselves; meanwhile, they've internalized put-downs and rejections, and tend to be harshly self-critical. As a result, they're less resilient, less able to cope with stress and setbacks. Deep down, connection needs do not feel sufficiently met, and they're prone to entering the Reactive mode in their relationships.

SECURE IN THE CORE OF YOUR BEING

Conceptual models need to make sharp distinctions, but reality is fuzzier. Secure and insecure attachment styles are at opposite ends of a range, like a color spectrum with bright green at one end and bright red at the other, and a lot of messy complexity in the middle. Wherever you are on this range, you can move toward a greater sense of security, both inside particular relationships and with people in general. The *plasticity* of the nervous system that makes us so easily affected by bad experiences in relationships also enables us to heal and grow from good ones, and to become more secure—more centered in the green zone with others—over time.

Take In Feeling Cared About

Experiences today may not have everything that would have been so good to have received as a child or adult, but at least they can offer part of what was missing for you. Caring comes in five major forms, with increasing intensity: being included, seen, appreciated, liked, and loved. Each one of these is an opportunity to feel cared about. Over time, repeatedly internalizing these experiences can build up a basis for secure attachment.

As you go through your day, look for the little moments in which another person is interested, friendly, grateful, empathic, respectful, affectionate, or loving. Other things may be happening in that relationship which are not so positive for you, but whatever is good for you is still real. Use the HEAL steps to turn the recognition of caring for you into an experience that you stay with for a few breaths or longer, taking it into yourself. Most of the times you do this will be brief and mild, though you can also have more intense experiences, such as a deep sense of closeness with your partner. Experience by experience, synapse by synapse, you'll be growing a core in yourself that feels valued, liked, and loved: a solid base for real confidence. And for a longer, sustained experience of this, try the practice in the box.

FEELING CARED ABOUT

Think of people who matter to you. Be mindful of what it's like to feel caring toward them. See some of the ways that it is good for them to feel cared about. Turn it around and consider that it is good for you to feel cared about and that it is normal and all right for you to want this.

Think of beings who care about you today, or who have cared about you in the past. They could be individuals, a group of people, a pet, or a spiritual consciousness. Any form of caring counts. Recognize the *fact* that you are currently cared about in various ways and that you have been cared about. Let your knowing of this fact become an experience of feeling included . . . seen . . . appreciated . . . liked . . . loved.

Focus on the sense of being cared about. If other thoughts and feelings come up, disengage from them and return attention to feeling cared about. Enrich this experience by protecting it and keeping it going. Feel it in your body, perhaps with a hand on your heart. Notice what feels reassuring, comforting, or enjoyable about this experience.

If you like, use the Link step to connect this sense of being cared about with feelings of being left out or mistreated, inadequate or ashamed. Imagine that you are receiving caring into soft, yearning, young places inside. Take caring into yourself like a soothing balm for hurts and wounds. Know that you are worth being cared about; let this knowledge spread inside you like light moving into shadows of self-doubt. As always with Linking, emphasize the positive material, drop the negative if it's too powerful, and finish by focusing only on positive material.

Develop a Coherent Narrative

Research has shown that people who were insecurely attached as children can develop secure attachment as adults. A key step is to develop a realistic, integrated, "coherent" account of what happened when you were young and how that affected you. This is a gradual process that can take many months, even years. I've been reflecting on my own childhood for a long time, and new things are still clarifying for me.

Imagine how a fair-minded and warmhearted person would tell the true story of your childhood, year by year, from your birth to when you left home. Think about your parents and other influential people in your life as complex individuals with different parts inside, pulling in different directions. Try to see pain, loss, stress, mistreatment, or trauma for what it was and how it landed on you. Also try to see the love, friendship, affection, loyalty, and support you received. Step back and consider the years unfolding, everything that happened, how you reacted, and why. See how your childhood, including adolescence, naturally left traces behind. See the strengths that were developed, and the wounds.

With compassion for yourself, try to be matter-of-fact about the whole story of your childhood. Look for the common humanity in it, the threads of it that are shared with others. No matter how fragmented and disturbing it might have been, you can find security in a coherent and clear understanding of it. To reflect on your childhood in a structured way, try the practice in the box.

REFLECTING ON YOUR CHILDHOOD

Adapt these questions to your own background. For many of them, you won't have specific recollections, but you could have a sense in your body or an intuition about the answer. You might also have a good guess from what you know about your childhood, perhaps from other people. Try to bring compassion to anything that is painful or upsetting.

What was the first year of life like for you? Were you born preterm? Did you have health issues? Were your parents sensitive to your needs? When you cried, what usually happened? Was either of your parents significantly affected by depression, alcohol, or relationship issues?

What was it like to be a toddler, and then a preschooler? When you said no, how did your parents react? If you had siblings, how did that affect you? What kind of relationship did your parents have with each other, and how did that affect your family?

What was it like in grade school? Did you feel popular? What kind of friends did you have? Did you feel included? Were you bullied? What was it like to be a teenager? Did you feel confident or insecure? How did the changes in your body affect you socially? How did you get along with your parents? Did you feel seen and supported by them?

Looking back, what else made a big difference for you? Perhaps a divorce, frequent moves, financial problems, major illness or death in the family, a sibling with special needs, or a larger context of poverty or prejudice? Did anything traumatic happen to you, including abuse, injury, or shocking loss? Were there any people who especially protected or nurtured you, such as a grandparent, teacher, or best friend?

How has all this affected you and your relationships? How are you still affected today?

Help Others Attach Securely to *You*

One of the amazing things about becoming a parent was that loving our kids wasn't good just for them. It also slowly repaired the wounds and empty places inside *me*. It's almost magical: by giving what we didn't get, we receive something good ourselves.

Some relationships are relatively superficial, while others are very deep, such as a profound connection with a life partner. In the context of whatever the relationship is, other people can feel secure with you when you are dependable, empathic, and caring. They may still need to deal with their own forms of insecure attachment, but at least you are doing your own part. This increases the odds that others will treat you reasonably well, giving you opportunities to have and internalize experiences that will add to a secure core inside you.

There is something mysteriously *reparative* about treating others as you wish to be treated yourself. It feels like a mending inside of what's been torn or tattered. It's also an affirmation that no matter what happened to you, your innermost being is intact. You can still be good to others, and you can still love.

DON'T THROW DARTS

Think of a time when someone mistreated you, and recall your immediate reactions. You could have experienced something like surprise, hurt, and anger. And then what happened inside your mind? A follow-on cascade of thoughts and feelings is very common. For example, as I have, you might have stayed awake at night thinking about what you wished you had said.

A One-Two Punch

This two-step process of initial and then secondary reactions was described as the *first and second dart* by the Buddha. The first dart is unavoidable physical or emotional discomfort and pain: a headache, the cramping of stomach flu, the sadness at losing a friend, the shock at being unfairly attacked in a meeting at work. The second dart is the one we throw ourselves, adding unnecessary reactions to the conditions of life and its occasional first darts. For example, second darts include getting really worried about a minor misunderstanding with another person, brooding about being slighted, and holding on to resentments and grudges. Second darts are the source of so much human suffering, especially in our relationships. They make us more upset than we need to be and cause us to do things we regret later.

To some extent, you can prevent first darts by changing the situations and relationships that affect you. For example, you might be able to find a less stressful job or spend less time with a difficult relative. Also, as we've been exploring in this book, you can develop an increasingly robust core of peace, contentment, and love that functions as an internal shock absorber. Then certain situations and relationships that used to be first darts for you will bother you less, if at all.

Yet many first darts still come to every person. When a first dart lands, it's there and you cannot change the fact of it. The brick has dropped on your foot and it hurts. Someone has yelled at you and you're startled and angry. You feel what you feel. When this happens, you can use the three major ways to engage the mind. First, *be with* the experience, riding it out mindfully, accepting it with a sense of curiosity and self-compassion. Second, *let go* of tension and emotions, and step away from unhelpful thoughts or desires. Third, try to *let in* whatever might be beneficial, replacing what you have released with something that's useful or enjoyable.

Practicing with Second Darts

Meanwhile, you can stop the first dart from triggering a salvo of second darts. This is where you can develop much influence over your own mind.

To begin with, you can have a sense of perspective about first darts in general. They're a natural and unavoidable part of life, and we don't need to add our reactions to them. If a Sunday picnic is ruined by a sudden thunderstorm, it's unfortunate and unpleasant, but there's no sense in yelling at the rain. If you accept the first dart for what it is, that's like a circuit breaker interrupting the flow of second darts.

In particular, it's useful to have perspective on first darts in relationships. For example, it's natural to care about how others see you. It's natural to feel unsettled if they are critical; this is the first dart. To leave it at that and not add second darts, here's a reflection about human evolution that's been very helpful to me.

Altruism—giving to others at personal cost—is very rare in the animal kingdom. In most species, freeloaders can take advantage of altruism, which lowers the chances of survival of generous individuals and thus suppresses the evolution of altruism in that species. Human altruism—helping strangers, jumping into a river to rescue someone else's dog—was able to develop because the evolving social brain enabled our ancestors to understand and care deeply about what others thought of them. Living in small groups, sometimes on the edge of starvation, a person's reputation was a life-and-death matter. Imagine being on the plains of Africa 100,000 years ago: if you shared your food with someone yesterday and then that person refused to share food with you today, everyone in the band would know about it, and no one would share food with that person again. Consequently, freeloaders could not get away with exploiting the generosity of others.

The priority that people place on what others think about them creates our vulnerability to embarrassment, hurt, and shame, but it is also what enables altruism. Similarly, our vulnerabilities to loneliness, envy, resentment, and indignation are necessary features of the deeply social human nature that also gives us friendship, compassion, love, and justice.

When you know this, first darts in relationships make more sense, so they don't seem as alarming. They're normal, a natural sort of pain. When you see that they've been shaped by millions of years of evolution, they don't feel so immediate and penetrating and personal. Painful as they are, they're in the service of a good cause. Experiencing them is a little like taking one for the human team.

Building on this sense of perspective about first darts, try to work with second dart reactions inside yourself. (Later chapters will address skillful ways to interact with *others*.) Take a breath, step back, and recognize second darts for what they are: needless suffering. Observe them revving up and see how they try to hijack your attention. If you're ruminating about an issue with someone, focus your attention on self-compassion. Then try to focus on experiencing key resources that are matched to the issue, such as bringing to mind people who do care about you. If you don't add fuel to second darts, they tend to run out of gas on their own. For example, if you stop building up a case in your mind about people who've wronged you, your resentments will probably fade into the background. In particular, watch out for the inner critic, a major thrower of second darts.

STAND UP TO THE INNER CRITIC

There are two different attitudes or "voices" inside us all, one that is nurturing and another that is critical, one that lifts up and one that weighs down. This is perfectly normal, not psychotic. Each of these parts of you has a role to play. The inner nurturer brings self-compassion and encouragement. The inner critic helps you recognize where you've gone wrong and what you need to do to set things right.

But for most people, the inner critic goes way overboard, throwing second dart after second dart of scolding, shaming, nit-picking, and faultfinding. It's big and powerful, while the inner nurturer is small and ineffective, which wears down mood, self-worth, and resilience. Happily, there are good ways to reset this balance by restraining the critic and strengthening the nurturer inside yourself.

Be Mindful of Self-Criticism

Try to observe how self-criticism operates inside you. Notice any dismissal or minimization of your pain, your needs, and your rights. Watch how little streams of thought downplay your accomplishments: "Oh, anyone could have done that . . . but it wasn't perfect . . . what about the other times when you messed up?" Observe any repetitive doubting or discouraging of your hopes and dreams. See if you're raining on your own parade. Be aware of anger at yourself that seems out of proportion to whatever happened, and listen inside for a tone of scolding, berating, or shaming—like someone is yelling at you. Recognize any underlying attitude that you always have to do more to be good enough. Identify any over-the-top moralistic self-condemnation: "You should be ashamed of yourself, you're a bad person."

As you observe what's happening in your mind, try to label it to yourself, such as: "self-criticism," "saying my pain doesn't matter," "lashing and lambasting again." See if there is anything familiar about the words, tone, or attitude in the self-criticism. Does it remind you of anyone, such as a parent, an older sibling, or a coach? Consider how self-critical attitudes developed inside you, perhaps when you were younger.

When you're mindful in these ways, you can learn about yourself and see the dogmatism, harshness, and absurdity in much of what the inner critic has to say. Stepping back from the criticism to observe it stops reinforcing it and helps you *disidentify* from it: you may have it, but you don't need to *be* it. And in your brain, you'll be associating a calm witnessing to the inner critic—a form of Linking—which can make it less intense and more reasonable.

Strengthen the Inner Nurturer

When the inner critic starts pounding away, the inner nurturer is a refuge and an ally. This part of yourself is protective and encouraging when other people are critical of you, and when things are stressful, disappointing, even terrible. It is a major source of confidence and resilience.

Starting in early childhood, we develop the inner nurturer by internalizing experiences with *outer* nurturers, such as parents, preschool teachers, and older children. But if external nurturance was spotty, or if it was compromised in some way—such as by having a parent who was both loving and intensely critical—then self-nurturance doesn't become as strong as it should be.

No matter what happened in your past, these days you can build up an inner nurturer by using the HEAL steps to internalize experiences in which others are caring toward you—growing a natural, lasting sense of caring for yourself from the inside out. Additionally, when you are caring toward yourself—such as telling yourself that a small mistake is not a big deal—then take in these experiences, which will strengthen your inner nurturer.

It may sound silly, but you could imagine a "caring committee" inside yourself with different characters on it who represent various kinds of support and wisdom. My caring committee includes my wife and kids, tough-but-kind rock climbing guides, several close friends, and even some fictional characters, such as Gandalf from *The Lord of the Rings*, Spock from *Star Trek*, and the plump fairy godmother from the story of Sleeping Beauty. Really! Who's on your own caring committee?

When the inner critic gets going or when life is challenging, call on the inner nurturer. Get to know the feeling of it, the sense of it in your body, the attitudes it has, the advice it gives you. You could start by recalling someone who's been very caring toward you, and then shift your attention to a more general feeling of being sheltered, comforted, or guided. And when you have a sense of the inner nurturer, focus on this experience and take it in: one more opportunity to reinforce the nurturer inside yourself.

Push Back Against the Critic

As soon as you recognize the characteristic tone or words of the inner critic, be skeptical about it. It's guilty until proven innocent. Make a fundamental choice about whether you want to join with it and believe it, or instead separate from it and doubt it. The inner critic usually gets more powerful when others have been nasty, belittling, or mean toward you. What they did to you was wrong, and it's not right to do it to yourself.

Argue against the inner critic—and truly intend to win. Write down one of its typical lines—such as "You always fail"—and then write down three or more believable rebuttals, such as some of the many times you have succeeded. Imagine members of your caring committee sticking up for you and talking back to the critic. Ally with *them*, not with it. Talk to yourself in useful ways, such as: "This criticism has a grain of truth in it, but everything else is exaggerated or untrue." "This is what ____ used to tell me; it was wrong then and it's wrong now." "This is not helping me and I don't have to listen to it."

Try regarding the inner critic as something that lacks credibility. You could imagine it as a ridiculous character, like a silly cartoon villain in a Disney movie. Place it "over there" in your mind, outside the core of your being, like that annoying person in a meeting who is always critical but whom everybody tunes out after a while.

Use the Link step to sense that reassurance and encouragement are sinking down into places inside that have been criticized and have felt inadequate or ashamed. Feel a soothing and calming spread inside you. Rest in a peaceful worth and confidence.

KNOW YOU'RE A GOOD PERSON

Think about someone who you feel is a basically good person. No need to be a saint. Just someone with a core of decency and caring. Then think about someone else you consider to be a basically good person. Notice how often you see good qualities in others, even people you don't know that well.

Turn it around, and understand that most people are like you. They, too, routinely recognize that someone is a basically good person. In fact, they routinely recognize that *you* are a basically good person.

Let it sink in that what you feel about others, they feel about *you*. They feel it because they see it. You're not tricking or fooling them. They know you have flaws and faults, and it doesn't matter. The key people in your life still think you are a basically good person.

Can you see yourself the way others see you, as essentially good and worthy? For many people, this is quite hard to do. Seeing *others* as good people seems straightforward. You might also recognize intellectually that others see your good intentions and warm heart. But seeing yourself in this way? It's oddly difficult for most of us. It can feel like a taboo of sorts—something that's just not allowed. But why not? If it's all right to recognize basic goodness in others, and it's all right for them to recognize it in you, why is it not all right to recognize it and stand up for it inside yourself?

As you go through your day, try to register it when others see decency, capability, effort, and caring in you—typically in small passing moments that are nonetheless real. Also recognize your own good qualities much as you would see them in others. Label them in your mind as a fair-minded observer would, such as: "trying hard," "being friendly," "admitting a mistake," "being skillful," "contributing," "enduring when things are hard," "giving love." Be aware of the integrity and lovingness deep inside you even if they're not always apparent or expressed. Let a sense of confidence in your inherent value grow and fill your mind. Let it sink in. Try to do this again and again.

Knowing in your heart that you are a basically good person is a true refuge. No matter the ups and downs of successes and failures, loves and losses, you can find comfort and strength in this knowledge. Independent of all achievements, fame, and fortune, there is always goodness in the core of your being.

KEY POINTS

- Humans evolved to be dependent upon each other. When others are dependably helpful and caring, especially when we are young, we develop a sense of security and internal stability. But if others are distant or rejecting, we feel insecure and become less resilient.

- No matter what has happened to you in the past, you can become more secure inside yourself. To do this, look for opportunities to feel cared about and take these experiences into yourself; develop a "coherent narrative" about your childhood; and be dependably empathic and caring toward others.

- When difficult things happen to us, we often add a second wave of reactions to the initial pain or upset. These second darts create so much of our suffering, especially in relationships. Try to be mindful of them, disengage from them, and stop fueling them.

- A major source of second darts is the inner critic. It tries to be helpful but goes overboard with scolding and shaming. This erodes self-worth and makes it harder to bounce back from disappointment or failure. Strengthen the inner nurturer and then push back against the inner critic.

- You routinely recognize that others are basically good persons. Well, they see that about you. Help yourself know that you are a basically good person. Whatever happens outside you or to you, the foundation of lasting confidence is the sure knowledge that there is goodness at the heart of you.

PART THREE

REGULATING

CHAPTER 7

CALM

You are the sky. Everything else—it's just the weather.

—Pema Chödrön

Forrest and I once went whitewater rafting on the Klamath River in Northern California. Our guide took us through steep drops that drenched us with spray, and it was tons of fun—plus a great lesson. The rapids were dangerous and challenged our need for safety. But I remember the guide's face: careful yet sure of himself, alert yet relaxed, as he handled the hazards around us. He had *calm*, the mental resource that helps us stay in the green zone as we deal with pain or the threat of it.

Everyone has physical or emotional pain some of the time, and many people experience it all of the time. Besides actual pain, threats of pain come from many directions, from trucks driving too close to your car to irritation flickering across the face of your partner. Even pursuing opportunities can bring the threat of pain. For example, one of the scariest experiences of my life was telling my first real girlfriend that I loved her while not knowing what she would say in return. (She said she loved me, too.)

When faced with pain or the threat of it, you might be able to stay calm like the guide. But it's common to be triggered into *flight*, *fight*, or *freeze* reactions, with some combination of:

- **Fear:** uneasiness, nervousness, worry, anxiety, alarm, panic

- **Anger:** exasperation, annoyance, irritation, indignation, rage

- **Helplessness:** overwhelm, impotence, defeat, futility, paralysis

It's normal to experience fear, anger, or helplessness from time to time. Problems arise when these reactions are invasive or chronic, or otherwise impact your well-being, relationships, or work. Because the need for safety is so vital, it's equally vital that we regulate ourselves to meet pain and threats with calm strength. To help you do this, we'll explore relaxing and centering, seeing threats accurately, feeling safer, and cooling anger. (For any feelings of helplessness, take a look back at the section on agency in Chapter 4.)

RELAXING AND CENTERING

As Alan Watts said, life is "wiggly." Inside the body and mind, things are continually changing, for better or worse. Plus we live in an increasingly volatile, uncertain, complex, and ambiguous world whose ripples surge through us each day.

The Healthy Resting State

To keep you on an even keel as you ride the inner and outer waves, the *autonomic* nervous system manages your body and mind through its *parasympathetic* and *sympathetic* branches. Think of these like the brake and gas pedals of a car. The "rest-and-digest" parasympathetic nervous system evolved first, before the sympathetic nervous system developed. When it is engaged, the heart rate slows down and the body refuels and repairs itself. Extreme parasympathetic activation can produce an intense freeze response, such as feeling like you can't speak, the human equivalent of an animal "playing dead." But normal parasympathetic activity feels good, with a sense of relaxed, centered well-being.

On the other hand, the sympathetic nervous system puts the pedal to the metal, mobilizing the body for action by speeding up the heart while hormones such as adrenaline and cortisol course through the blood. As the body revs up, so does the mind, with more intense thoughts and feelings. As we'll see in the next chapter, sympathetic activation is a wonderful source of passion and resilience when it's combined with positive emotions such as happiness, love, and confidence. The healthy resting state of your body and mind involves substantial parasympathetic activity with just enough sympathetic activation to keep things interesting. But when the sympathetic nervous system is combined with negative emotions such as anger or fear, these fight-or-flight reactions are stressful and upsetting. They burden your body and mind, and strain your relationships.

Unfortunately, our modern, go-go-go culture routinely pushes people into sympathetic nervous system overdrive with few opportunities for sustained parasympathetic recovery. There can also be individual reasons for sympathetic activation, such as having a driven personality or being on edge as a result of past trauma. Many of us experience chronic mild to moderate stress, living much of the time in a kind of "pink zone."

A person could slow down and do less. But the realities of work and family usually make this hard to achieve. If you are going to stay busy while juggling many balls and plates, it helps to keep engaging the parasympathetic wing of the nervous system along the way. One of the best ways to do this is through frequent practices of relaxation.

Settling Down

The parasympathetic and sympathetic branches of the nervous system are connected like a seesaw: if one goes up, the other is pushed down. As you relax, parasympathetic activation increases, which decreases sympathetic activity and related stress hormones. If you use the HEAL steps to internalize repeated experiences of relaxation, your baseline sense of life will become less pressured, anxious, or irritable. Then if you do start to feel tense or upset, you'll be able to return more quickly to a calm and centered place inside.

Relaxation comes easily when we're at leisure, such as walking in the woods. But that's not the only time we can feel it—or need it. A basketball player shooting a free throw in overtime must be able to relax and let muscle memory take over. In even more extreme situations, as Adam Savage put it, "calm people live, tense people die."

I learned this myself when I nearly drowned at age sixteen, skin diving in the Pacific Ocean. After holding my breath as long as I could, I tried to swim back up through a patch of kelp, but the seaweed snared me. I panicked and fought it, but just got more tangled up. I was running out of air and was sure I would die. Then from somewhere came a thought I remember to this day: "Cool it." I relaxed. My thrashing had ripped the snorkel out of my mouth, the mask was around my neck, and I'd lost a fin. I'd been underwater a long time. Still, I moved slowly to disentangle myself, working my way up through the orange-brown kelp. Finally I cleared it and rose to the silver-bright surface and a welcome gulp of air. There are some things about that experience I don't fully understand, including what said "Cool it." But the value of relaxation could not have been clearer.

To establish a calmer baseline for yourself plus recover more quickly after stress, set aside a few minutes or more to relax deeply many times a week. Also look for little moments to relax in the flow of your day, especially when the needle of your personal stress-o-meter starts creeping up into yellow, orange, or red. In our over-heated culture, relaxation needs to be a conscious priority. Many things are soothing and settling, and most can be used for longer or shorter periods. Here are some good ways to relax, and you can use the HEAL steps to take in these experiences.

EXTEND THE EXHALATION

The parasympathetic nervous system (PNS) manages exhaling and slows your heart rate, while the sympathetic nervous system handles inhaling and speeds up the heart. If you lengthen your exhalation, that naturally engages the PNS. For several breaths or more, try counting softly in your mind to make your exhalation longer than your inhalation. For example, inhale for 1-2-3 and then exhale for 1-2-3-4-5-6.

RELEASE TENSION

Pick a key region such as your jaw muscles or the diaphragm under your rib cage, bring awareness to the area, and deliberately relax it. You could imagine breathing into this area, or that light or energy is flowing through it and carrying tension away. If you like, try *progressive relaxation*, in which you start at your feet and move up to your head, systematically releasing tension in each major part of your body; you can also start at your head and move downward.

TRY BIOFEEDBACK

Various products use wearables or clips on an earlobe or finger to track your heart rate and breathing. Using real-time feedback from your body, you're guided to a calmer place, and you can see your progress over time. Some of these products aim at improving *heart rate variability*, the change in the interval between heartbeats, which reflects the degree to which your heart rate slows as you exhale and engage the PNS. Increased variability is a marker of greater parasympathetic activation in general, and is associated with improved mood, a stronger immune system, and greater resilience to stress.

MOVE

Yoga, t'ai chi, qigong, walking meditation, dancing, singing, and other structured forms of movement are relaxing and often energizing as well. You could also pick a routine activity, such as raking leaves or folding laundry, and do it in a very calm and easygoing way while staying in touch with your body.

USE IMAGERY

Much of our stress is driven by internal verbal processes. These worry about the future, rehash the past, and mutter about the present. In most people, the neural basis for language is on the left side of the brain while the right side handles imagery and other forms of holistic processing. (This is reversed for many left-handed people.) The two sides inhibit each other, so if one becomes more active, that quiets the other. Consequently, focusing on imagery will reduce verbal activity—and help you relax.

There are many ways to explore imagery. You could recall a beautiful place you have visited, and walk through it again in your mind. Imagine being in a relaxing situation, such as sitting by a lake or walking down a country road. Think back on a setting you felt good in, such as your grandparents' home, and recall as many details about it as possible. You could visualize fluffy white clouds—and soaring happily through them like a bird.

RECOGNIZING PAPER TIGER PARANOIA

Sometimes fear is obvious, such as feeling nervous or panicked. But much of the time, fear operates behind the scenes and exercises a hidden power. For example, fear is at work when a person stays within a small comfort zone, procrastinates to avoid a challenge, feels emotionally inhibited, or avoids speaking up and standing out.

Fear is so powerful because it's so fundamental to survival. The ways that we experience and try to cope with seemingly minor concerns today are shaped by the same neurohormonal machinery that helped our ancestors react to lethal threats and survive another day.

The Two Mistakes

As the nervous system evolved, animals could—metaphorically speaking—make two kinds of mistakes:

1. Believe there is a tiger in the bushes when there isn't one

2. Believe there is no tiger when one is about to pounce

In the wild, what's the cost of the first mistake? Needless anxiety, which is uncomfortable but not fatal. What's the cost of the second mistake? A good chance of death. Consequently, our ancestors developed a strong tendency to make the first mistake again and again in order to avoid making the second mistake even once. In effect, we're adaptively paranoid of paper tigers.

As a result, most people overestimate threats while underestimating their resources for managing them. These biases operate in the background and are often hard to see, which makes them very powerful. I had been a dorky and shy kid in school, and as an adult I just took it for granted that if I stood out in a group, bad things would happen. It was a long time before I became aware of this assumption and realized that most people aren't mean and rejecting.

Once a bias is established, we focus on and internalize the information and experiences that confirm it while ignoring or downplaying whatever might contradict it. Until I started to understand my own biased expectations about groups, the many times I was warmly included "didn't count," while the few times I was brushed aside seemed to prove that my fears had been justified all along.

Needless Anxiety

It's obviously important to recognize real threats and develop resources for handling them. But most people feel more anxious than is necessary or helpful. We tend to see ourselves, the world around us, and the future through fear-colored glasses. Even when you know rationally that there is absolutely nothing to fear, there is still often a background trickle of anxiety, a sense that something *could* go wrong at any minute. Anxiety functions as a signal of danger, but much of the time it is only noise, like a car alarm that's stuck, blaring away, unpleasant but meaningless.

And what are the costs? Anxiety feels bad, and it's stressful and fatiguing. Flooded with false alarms, it's easy to miss real threats, especially those that grow slowly over time, such as an emotional distance creeping into a marriage. Feeling anxious, we can overreact and become threatening to others, who overreact themselves and confirm our fears. Needless fear makes us shift resources from approaching opportunities to avoiding exaggerated threats. Anxiety increases defensiveness, paralysis by analysis, and immobilization. In relationships, fear makes people cling more tightly to "us" while being more suspicious and aggressive toward "them." All of this makes a person less resilient.

FEELING SAFER

Fear arises when threats seem bigger than resources. Sometimes this is actually the case, such as getting an unexpected bill that you don't have the money to pay. But due to "paper tiger paranoia," threats often look larger than they really are while resources look smaller than they really are.

Even if you realize that fear plays an irrationally large role in your life, it can still be hard to let go of it. Many people are afraid, in effect, of not being afraid, since that's when their shields are lowered. Then they fear that *whap*—something might hurt them.

To *be* safer, we need to decrease actual threats and increase actual resources. To *feel* safer, we need to stop inflating threats and start recognizing all our resources. Then we don't have to be afraid of not being afraid.

Let's say you're doing what you can to reduce the actual threats in your life while developing real resources for handling them. Meanwhile, make sure you are seeing threats clearly, appreciating your resources, and feeling as safe as you reasonably can.

Seeing Threats Clearly

Pick one thing that worries you. It could be an illness, finances, or a conflict with another person. It could also be an area of life in which you're holding back to reduce risks, such as avoiding public speaking or not asking for what you really want in a relationship. You can do this process by reflecting to yourself, journaling, or talking about it with someone, and you can use it with multiple things that worry you.

HOW BIG IS IT?

Be specific and concrete about the size of the challenge. In effect, put a fence around the issue rather than letting it be nebulous and overwhelming. For instance, instead of "My health is bad," how about "I have high blood pressure"? Bound the issue in space and time. What part of your life does it affect—and what is unaffected? When does it happen—and when is it not very relevant?

HOW LIKELY IS IT?

Perhaps you're stuck with an ongoing condition, such as a chronic health issue. But most of the time when we feel anxious, it's about something bad that *might* happen: there is a threat of pain, but not pain itself. For instance, a person might think, "I could get sick" or "If I express anger, no one will want me." If what you are concerned about is a possibility but not yet a reality, ask yourself: "What are the odds, actually?" In your past, a certain kind of bad event could indeed have been likely, perhaps because of the people you lived with or knew back then. But today, things are different, and the chances of a bad event are probably much lower.

HOW BAD WOULD IT ACTUALLY BE?

What would you *experience* if the threat did come true? Let's say you're afraid of someone rejecting you if you're more vulnerable or assertive. OK, suppose the feared event occurs. What would you actually feel if it happened? On a 0–10 scale, with 10 being the absolute worst imaginable, how bad would you feel? And for how long? In the past, similar events could have felt truly horrible, especially during childhood when things are felt more keenly before the nervous system fully matures. But these days, as an adult, you have many more inner shock absorbers. There's a good chance that you wouldn't feel as bad or for as long as you fear you would.

LET THE GOOD NEWS LAND

Let all this sink in. It is really, *really* true. You can believe it. Let yourself feel convinced of it. Using the HEAL steps, open to relief and reassurance about this good news. Take it into yourself, easing and gradually replacing excessive, needless alarm and tension and anxiety.

Appreciating Your Resources

Then ask yourself this: given the actual magnitude of the thing you fear, the odds of it happening, and the intensity of its impact, how could you cope with it? For example, suppose you discover a flat tire on your car. It's a hassle for sure. But it's not such a big problem if you know how to change a tire or if you can call a tow truck.

RESOURCES IN YOUR MIND

Think about times when you've drawn on inner strengths such as grit, confidence, and compassion to handle issues in the past. Then take some moments to consider how you could tap into those inner strengths again to deal with the current challenge. Also consider the talents and skills that you could bring to bear. How could you work on the problem? What plans could you make to prevent it, manage it, or recover from it? Think about other resources inside yourself—such as mindfulness and your own good heart—and how these could help you.

RESOURCES IN YOUR BODY

How has your body served you so far? How could it serve you again?
See if you can tune into its natural vitality. Feel what *is* strong about
it, energetic, and capable. Imagine some of the ways that your body
could help you with this challenge.

RESOURCES IN YOUR WORLD

There are many resources around you such as friends, family, and
acquaintances. How could they be useful? Consider both concrete
help and emotional support. Think about a pet if you have one; my
worries always felt lighter with our cat in my lap. If need be, could
you get professional help, perhaps from a doctor, lawyer, or accoun-
tant? Think about the things you own, and consider how you could
use them for this challenge.

FEELING DEEPLY RESOURCED

As you reflect on these resources, let your thoughts about them become feelings of enoughness, reassurance, and relief. Use the HEAL
steps to enrich and absorb these feelings. If you like, use the Link
step to use these positive feelings to soothe and replace any sense of
anxiety.

Feeling as Safe as You Reasonably Can

After one of my first days of rock climbing, I had a weird experience when I went to sleep. Suddenly and vividly, I was falling off the
top of the cliff and plummeting down to smash into gray granite. I
jerked awake before hitting it. After a few minutes, I drifted off—
and was again falling to my death, waking up just before impact.

After this happened several times, I stopped trying to fight it. As I slid into drowsiness, I let myself imagine that I was tumbling down the face of the cliff to splatter on a slab at the bottom. At the instant of impact, a kind of inner lightbulb went off. It dawned on me that I'd spent the day shoving down all of my fears of falling and they were now boiling back up. I realized there was a sweet spot in which I could feel appropriate anxiety while also functioning effectively and happily—even a thousand feet off the ground.

It's important not to suppress fear or overlook what it's trying to tell you. Reasonable concerns are your friend, keeping you out of potentially dangerous situations. But being consumed, invaded, and compromised by fear doesn't make you safer. If anything, the distractions of excessive fear and its wear and tear on the body actually undermine your safety. A little fear goes a long way, and it doesn't have to penetrate your core and push you into the red zone. One of my favorite sayings from the Buddha is "Painful feelings arose, but they did not invade my mind and remain." Use fear; don't let it use you.

And as we've seen, there need not be much fear at all. Most of the time, the threats we imagine aren't as likely as we think they are, their consequences won't be so bad, and we'd be more able to cope than we give ourselves credit for. It's like walking around believing that the world is at Threat Level Orange when in fact it's more like Threat Level Chartreuse: a bucket of green paint with a drop of yellow. If you're about to fall off a cliff—or the equivalent—sure, be afraid. But otherwise, repeatedly help yourself feel as safe as you reasonably can as you move through your day. To deepen this experience, try the practice in the box.

FEELING SAFER NOW

Take some breaths, and relax. Be mindful of any tension, uneasi-ness, or worry. Step back from any anxiety and observe it. Let it be, and let it come and go.

Let fear in any form move to the background of awareness. In the foreground, bring to mind things that protect you. Be aware of the solidity of the floor beneath your feet, the stability of a chair, the sheltering of a roof over your head. Be aware of your clothing, shoes, and other things that protect you. As you recog-nize these protections, open to feeling increasingly protected. Be aware of things around you that are protective, such as stop signs and hospitals. Keep opening to feeling protected. Allow a sense of protection and safety to sink in, becoming a part of you.

Recognize some of the many resources in your life that could help you be safe, such as people who wish you well, who would stand with you and for you. Also resources inside you, such as en-durance and determination. Open to feeling that there is a lot you can draw on. Challenges will come, but you've got many ways to deal with them. Keep opening to feeling safer. Let needless worry fall away. Let go of any tension. Let a sense of safety sink in and spread inside you.

Notice that you are basically all right, right now. You may not have been all right in the past, and you may not be all right in the future, but in this moment you are OK, protected, and resourced. There may be pain, there may be hurt or sorrow off to the edges of your mind. But there is no mortal threat, no tiger about to pounce. You are fundamentally safe, moment after moment, breath after breath. Your heart is still beating, you are going on living, you are still all right. Let thoughts and feelings come and go. Abide with ease at the front edge of now. You are still breathing just fine, the next moment is passing through, you're still OK, you're safe now, safe in this moment, moment after moment, basically all right, right . . . now.

COOLING ANGER

Anger is a natural response to pain, frustration, attack, and injustice. As someone who grew up in a home in which the parents had a monopoly on anger, it took me a while to learn that experiencing and expressing this emotion was an important way to accept and stand up for myself. Throughout history, different kinds of people—such as children, women, and religious and ethnic groups—have had their justifiable anger brushed aside, explained away, or attacked. It's especially important to make room in your mind for anger if others have tried to banish it.

Anger mobilizes energy and shines a bright light on whatever is at issue. Nonetheless, anger also comes wrapped with tension, stress, and threats to relationships. Frequent or chronic anger is fatiguing; like hot acid, it eats away at physical and mental health. Of all the emotions we express to each other, anger usually compels the most attention, like a red light flashing "danger." Then we react to the other person's anger with our own anger, creating vicious cycles in relationships.

Cooling down anger does not mean enabling injustice or turning into a patsy. You can still be strong and forceful. Think of times when you or others were determined, passionate, or assertive while not being swept away with anger. The art is to receive and use the gift—the positive functions of anger—while being careful about the wrapper. This means managing and expressing anger in skillful ways while also addressing the issues that underlie it.

Be Mindful of Anger

Anger is often at work in the back of the mind, and recognizing its presence enables you to control it rather than it controlling you. Try to be aware of anger in its many shades and intensities, from mild exasperation to violent rage. When you feel angry in any way, explore the experience, including its sensations, feelings, thoughts, and desires. Anger is layered, and its brittle, hot, aggressive surface usually rests on a soft, vulnerable, anxious foundation of unmet needs—especially safety, since anger is a primal reaction to threat. Anger is a messenger. What is it telling you about your deeper frustrations, unfulfilled longings, and emotional pain? Try to accept your experience and have compassion for yourself. As you open to and be with this deeper material, anger itself tends to let go.

Beware the rewards that come with anger. There are four major types of "negative" emotions: sadness, anxiety, shame, and anger. Of them, anger is the most seductive. Most people don't enjoy feeling glum, worried, or inadequate. But the surge of righteous indignation and energy that comes with anger can feel stimulating, organizing (as it draws together the threads of a scattered mind and identifies a clear target), and even pleasurable. Anger is also an effective way to hide hurt and vulnerability, assert status or dominance, push away fear, and compensate for feeling small or weak. In relationships, arguing or bickering can serve the purpose of keeping others at a comfortable distance. A saying describes anger as a poisoned barb with a honeyed tip. I've spent more hours than I'd like to admit tasting that honey while ruminating angrily about how I'd been wronged. Meanwhile, the poison was seeping in, stressing and upsetting me while priming me to overreact in the future.

Try to be mindful of the process of getting angry, which typically happens in two stages: the *priming* and the *trigger*. In the first stage, little things add up. Some are general, including stress, weariness, and hunger. Others are more specific, such as the small moments of feeling misunderstood, let down, or hassled that gradually sensitize you to a particular person. It's like someone dragging a fingernail across the back of your hand: the first dozen times don't matter much, but by the hundredth time it happens, you naturally flinch and pull back. Even minor experiences can build up like a pile of unlit matches.

Then, in the second stage, some kind of spark lands and starts a fire—often way out of proportion to the trigger itself. For example, when our kids were young and cluttering the floor with their toys and shoes, if I was in a good mood I hardly noticed their stuff. But if I was tired at the end of a frustrating day (the priming) and stubbed my toe on a fire truck (the trigger), *kaboom!* In the moment of being angry, we tend to presume that it is justified by whatever happened: "Well, of *course* I'm mad!" But usually, most of the anger has been fueled by the priming and is out of proportion to the trigger itself.

Be Skillful with Anger Inside Yourself

In Chapter 10, "Courage," we'll explore how to assert yourself effectively. Here I would like to focus on how to deal with anger inside your own mind. Then, when you do communicate with others, things are likely to go better.

RECOGNIZE HOW ANGER HURTS YOU

There's a proverb that says: Getting angry at others is like throwing hot coals with bare hands—both people get burned. Because anger can feel both rewarding and justified, it helps to realize that it is a toxic burden on *you*, in addition to its consequences for others.

Take some time to consider the costs of anger for you personally, both these days and over the past years of your life. Think about how it makes you feel. Think about its effects on your sleep, body, and health, and its effects on your relationships at home or work. Even when anger is kept inside, it eats away at a person. You may have heard it said that resentment is like taking poison and waiting for others to die.

After reflecting on all this, decide in your heart how you want to relate to and manage anger. Decide how you want to address its underlying causes, such as physical pain or being mistreated by others. And decide how you want to express it. Help yourself have a sense of conviction about these decisions, and take in this sense of commitment.

REDUCE THE PRIMING

Over the course of your day, be aware of the run-up to anger, and intervene early as best you can. For example, take a break to clear your head from work before talking about homework with your teenager or remind yourself to be extra careful with your words when your back is hurting. Recognize if you've become sensitized to a person, setting, or topic. If you have, name it to yourself so it has less power over you, such as "I'm edgy about visiting the in-laws again," "I've had it up to here with being constantly interrupted in this meeting," or "I'm frustrated that nobody helps with the dishes."

When things do go awry, try to react in proportion to the trigger itself, without the amplifying effect of the priming. Ask yourself how you'd react if the trigger—the situation, event, words, or tone—were happening for the first time. Put the trigger in perspective. On your this-is-bad scale running from 0 to 10, how bad is the trigger, really? How long will its effects last? Will you even remember it in a couple of days? This is not about minimizing the trigger, but about seeing it clearly. It has helped me so many times to realize that what had happened was in fact a 2 but my anger was surging to a 7. When I recognized this, I could be with the hot wave of over-reactions while also keeping my own words and tone as close to a 2 as possible. Then after you've dealt with the trigger itself, you can address what has caused the priming.

DISENGAGE FROM RIGHTEOUSNESS

It's useful to have values and standards. But if you add righteousness to them, with its dogmatism and superiority, this adds fuel to your anger, triggers reactions from others, and undermines your credibility. The righteous case we develop about people is like a river in a flood carrying the boat of anger.

In your mind, try to separate any all-knowingness or "I'm better than you" from the actual heart of the matter. For example, it's one thing to want roommates to do their dishes, but it's something else to think they're lazy, selfish slackers if they don't. Recognize what righteousness is like as an experience—perhaps with a tightening around your eyes and prosecutorial acceleration of thought—so that warning lights flash on your inner dashboard when it starts to come over you. Because righteousness can feel good, remember how you don't like it when others get righteous with you, and use this to motivate yourself to set down that angry barb even if its tip might at first seem sweet.

Imagine describing the issue firmly and fully—including how it's affected you and what you wish would change—without the topspin of righteousness. Keep this fair-minded account of things in mind, and whenever it's appropriate, you can choose to share it with others.

BE CAREFUL ABOUT FAULTFINDING

I grew up in a faultfinding home. Because of their own upbringing, my mother and father worried about things going wrong and were therefore quick to point out the mistakes of others. They had truly good intentions and were just trying to help. Nonetheless, I became defensive when criticized, and I acquired the habit of looking for faults in other people—especially those I was angry with. Understandable as this has been, it's created needless tension and conflict in my relationships.

Pick an important relationship, and see if your mind tends to scan for errors, words to take issue with, nits to pick. Then ask yourself, "How much of this *really* matters?" Much of what bothers people does not directly harm them or those they care about. There's a Zen story that illustrates this. A senior monk and a junior monk with strict vows of celibacy were on a journey and came upon a beautiful woman at the edge of a muddy river. The older monk offered to carry her across, she gratefully accepted, and he did so. Then she went on her way. Afterward, the two monks continued on their path. For the next hour, the younger one kept obsessing to himself: *How could he have held her warm soft body in his arms, feeling her sweet breath upon his neck? How terrible that he kept smelling her beautiful long hair!* Finally he confronted the other man and burst out with what he'd been thinking. The senior monk listened, then smiled gently and said, "I set her down on the other side of the river, but you've been carrying her ever since." If you've grown preoccupied with the faults and failings of others, imagine how good it would feel to set these down.

SLOW IT DOWN

In your brain, information flows along multiple major paths like the branching and intertwining channels of a river. A key pathway of incoming information goes through the subcortical sensory switchboard, the thalamus, and then it forks. One branch connects to the amygdala, the brain's ancient alarm bell (among other functions). The other branch leads to the recently evolved prefrontal cortex, which is the center of complex thought, careful planning, and nuanced understanding of other people.

Located next to the thalamus, the amygdala gets a head start over the prefrontal cortex. Its "jump first, think later" nature drives our immediate reactions. The amygdala also biases the interpretations and analysis of the prefrontal cortex when it starts catching up a second or two or three later. This is the *amygdala hijack* in action: great for raw survival, but also the source of much needless upset, overheated reactions, and painful conflicts with others. In my own relationships and in the couples I've counseled in my office, I've seen so many runaway interactions in which A reacts to B, who reacts to A, who then overreacts to B, who then really overreacts to A, and on and on.

Things go much better if you slow them down. Give yourself—and the other person—the gift of time: time to take a breath or two, figure out what the other person is really saying, allow the first waves of fight-or-flight reactions to pass through your body, and recognize and restrain impulsive words and actions that you'll regret later. Those extra seconds before you speak help others feel less like they're on the receiving end of a rat-a-tat-tat barrage of words and emotional intensity. And the extra seconds give *them* time to reflect and be less hijacked themselves.

If you need to, disengage and cool off. For example, look out the window, get something to eat, or go for a walk. You're not trying to stonewall an issue but to settle down so you can engage it productively. Then, an hour or a day later, you can come back to it.

TRY NOT SPEAKING OR ACTING FROM ANGER

This doesn't mean not *feeling* angry. Anger is natural, and it indicates needs that don't feel met. Suppressing it usually creates more problems than solutions. Nor does this mean that you must *never* come from anger. I think there are times when people need anger to fight for their lives—or for the lives of others.

With this in mind, as an experiment, you could commit for a day to not speaking or acting from anger. I've tried this myself and it has helped me slow down, tune into the hurt or worry beneath my anger, and then talk in a more heartfelt and less critical or pushy way. You can still feel the anger, acknowledge what you're feeling to others, and address whatever is at issue. Meanwhile, see what it's like to separate out the anger from everything else in your mind and not let it be the controlling force behind what you say or do.

• • •

Pain or the threat of it comes to us all, challenging our need for safety. From time to time, fear and anger in all their forms surge through everyone's mind. With the strength of calm, you can handle these currents much like a rafting guide riding a river in full flood.

KEY POINTS

- Two branches of the nervous system work together to keep us on an even keel. The "rest-and-digest" parasympathetic branch settles us down, while the "fight-or-flight" sympathetic branch revs us up.

- The pace of modern life fosters chronic sympathetic activation, which is stressful for your body, mind, and relationships. So look for regular opportunities to engage the parasympathetic nervous system, such as relaxation or meditation.

- We react to imaginary or exaggerated threats to prevent ever missing a real one. It's a kind of "paper tiger paranoia" that creates needless anxiety plus makes it harder to see and cope with actual threats.

- Look for ways you could be overestimating threats while underestimating resources to deal with them. Notice that you are basically all right, right now. Help yourself feel as safe as you reasonably can.

- Anger puts a lot of wear and tear on your body and mind, and it feeds conflicts with others. You can be powerful and assertive without being angry.

- Anger comes in two stages: the priming and the trigger. Try to act early to reduce the priming and respond to the trigger in proportion to it. Be careful about self-righteousness and fault-finding, and slow down interactions to prevent an "amygdala hijack."

CHAPTER 8

MOTIVATION

Wisdom is choosing a greater
happiness over a lesser one.

—The Buddha

Resilience is more than managing stress and pain and recovering from loss and trauma. People who are resilient are also able to pursue opportunities in the face of challenges. They are able to start doing things that are beneficial, to stop doing things that are harmful, and to keep on going day after day without getting too stressed about it.

To be resilient in this way, we need to regulate the motivational machinery in our brains. So let's explore how to enjoy pleasures without getting attached to them, draw on healthy passion, and be motivated in positive directions. Broadly speaking, this chapter is about *desire*, an inherent feature of embodied life. We cannot end desire. Wishing that beings not suffer is a desire. Even the desire to transcend desire is itself a desire. The only question is, can we desire *well*?

LIKING AND WANTING

Imagine having dinner at a friend's home and stuffing yourself with a fantastic meal, including two desserts. They bring out another dessert and give you a taste and ask, "Do you like it?" Naturally, you say, "Yes, it's delicious." Then they ask, "Do you want some?" And you reply, "No thank you, I'm absolutely full!" You like, but you don't want.

Now imagine someone at a slot machine, putting in a quarter and pulling the lever, over and over. I've watched many people in casinos, and they usually look tired and bored, hardly smiling at the occasional payoff. There's a compulsive persistence but little enjoyment. They want, but they don't like.

In other words, liking and wanting are distinct experiences. They are also distinct neurologically. As one example of this, deep inside the basal ganglia in your subcortex, a region called the *nucleus accumbens* contains a small node that helps regulate the sense of liking something and a separate node that regulates the sense of wanting it.

The Tipping Point

I'm using the word "wanting" in a narrowly specific way in this chapter, as a state of insistence, drivenness, or craving that's based on an underlying sense of deficit and disturbance. The root of this word means *"lack."* It's natural to like things that are pleasurable, such as a sweet dessert with friends. But issues arise as we move from liking to wanting, from enjoying a meal together to insisting on the last piece of pie.

The shift from liking to wanting marks the tipping point from the green zone to the red zone, from an underlying feeling of fullness and balance to a sense of something lacking, something wrong. It's extremely useful to become aware of this transition in real time. Then you can shift back into simply liking, and pursue opportunities and enjoy pleasures without adding the stress that comes from wanting.

There's a saying that liking without wanting is heaven, but wanting without liking is hell. When you like something without wanting it, you're able to enjoy it fully. There is no tension around the experience, no holding on to it or fearing when it will end. In the moment, there is freedom from want. Then your beneficial experiences tend to last longer and feel more rewarding. This naturally engages the Enriching and Absorbing steps in the HEAL process, which increases the installation of the experience in your nervous system. We learn more and gain more from our experiences when we simply like them.

Henry David Thoreau wrote, "I make myself rich by making my wants few." There are many benefits in staying centered in liking without tipping into wanting. But it's often challenging. Consumerism is a driver of modern economies, and sometimes it seems like the greatest minds of our generation are busy devising ever more effective ways to stimulate wanting. Further, even if we turn off the TV, get off social media, and never walk through a mall, we have a brain that's designed to *want what it likes.*

Wanting More

The innate tendencies of the mind—our human nature—are the result of several hundred million years of sculpting the brain. Competing with others for scarce resources, our ancestors evolved motivational systems that pushed them into intense pursuit of goals such as food or sex. This was good for survival, but one of the results today is a kind of inner advertising agency that tries to motivate you by routinely overselling how good it will be if you get what you want.

As you weigh different choices, look forward to an event, or think about a particular goal, be mindful of the anticipated rewards your mind is forecasting. Then notice what the *actual* rewards turn out to be. Much of the time, they're less than what was promised. Additionally, even when the experience lives up to expectations, it ends eventually. The meal was nice, the new sweater looked good, it was gratifying to finish the project at work. But then the experience is gone. Now what?

Anticipated rewards are frequently disappointing. Even the best experiences are impermanent. These two facts can create a chronic sense that something is missing, something is wanting. This pushes us to keep seeking the next shiny object, the next experience.

Even when you're feeling at ease, with no problem to solve and no need for anything else, see if you can notice a kind of *auto-wanting* in the back of your mind: an ongoing scanning for something new to want even when you are already satisfied. This tendency may have evolved to prod our ancestors into foraging and sniffing about for new opportunities. But embedded in this auto-wanting is also an underlying feeling of restlessness and a subtle sense that the moment, every moment, is never fully satisfactory as it is.

This hunger for the next thing pulls us away from appreciating what we have and toward wanting what we lack. It's poignant that we habitually seek satisfaction with a mindset shaded with dissatisfaction, which holds complete contentment always just out of reach.

Liking Without Wanting

There are times when a person must move into a state of intense wanting in order to meet immediate needs. Some years ago a brushfire began in the hills above our home. I knew we might be ordered to evacuate on short notice and it was possible that our house would be threatened. I ran inside and quickly gathered up the essentials we wanted to have with us just in case. My heart was racing and the adrenaline was pumping. It was a necessary spike of red zone stress. And then it settled back down into orange, yellow, and green as we watched the fire department put out the fire before it spread any farther. Sometimes wanting is necessary. But it always comes with costs, from a subtle experience of tension and contraction to long-term wear and tear on your body and relationships. To meet life from a sense of liking without wanting, the methods below are really effective.

BE MINDFUL OF THE HEDONIC TONE

Be aware of the sense of experiences as being pleasant, unpleasant, or neutral. This is their *hedonic tone*. We like and approach things that have a pleasant hedonic tone, dislike and avoid things that are unpleasant, and ignore or move on from things that are neutral. Also be aware of the hedonic tone of the different things you *imagine* doing, such as planning a meeting, thinking about how to approach a difficult conversation, or deciding whether to buy something.

We tend to move rapidly into wanting things that have a pleasant hedonic tone. Consequently, mindfulness of the hedonic tones of your experiences creates a space between the pleasantness of an experience and any wanting related to it. In that space, you have a choice, and you don't have to shift automatically into wanting.

EXPLORE SIMPLY LIKING

See what it feels like to enjoy something distinct from wanting it. Be aware of a sense of ease in your body. Observe how your thoughts remain open and flexible. Notice that you can enjoy something without adding the stressful drivenness of wanting to it.

Become familiar with the sense of having pleasure—savoring a meal, laughing with friends—while letting go of any wanting about it. Repeatedly take in this way of relating to the things you enjoy so that it becomes increasingly natural for you.

EXPLORE THE EXPERIENCE OF WANTING

As you go through your day, be mindful of the transition from en-joyably liking something to stressfully wanting it. Be aware of "auto-wanting" in the back of your mind, looking for something new to want even when you already feel fine. Recognize sales pitches from your inner ad agency which might seem like: "It will taste/feel/be so good." "Don't worry, just one more time." "No one will know." "It will be so much fun." Then, when you do experience what you wanted, notice when it's not as good as promised.

Imagine a kind of inner dashboard and notice when red lights of wanting start flashing on it. Get to know different "flavors" of wanting. For example, be mindful of what it's like to feel urgent, pressured, contracted, insistent, demanding, compelled, craving, or addicted. Step back and observe the elements of an experience of wanting: the thoughts and images, bodily sensations, emotions, facial expressions, posture, and actions. Notice how wanting feels different from liking.

Recognize that wanting is an experience like any other, made up of parts that come and go. Try to see experiences of wanting as clouds moving through the sky of awareness. Then they don't feel so weighty, thing-like, and compelling.

Notice the beginnings of pressure, insistence, and other indi-cators of wanting. Also notice the persuasions and sometimes ma-nipulations of others who try to get you to want things—usually for their own sake, not yours.

COME BACK TO LIKING

The fact that wanting arises in awareness is not itself a problem. It is natural to want. The problem is that we privilege experiences of wanting and let them control us. Just because there is an experience of wanting does not mean you *have* to do something. The crux is not whether wanting arises but what your relationship to it is.

Recognize the costs of wanting for your health, well-being, and relationships. See if you can make a fundamental choice to engage life as much as possible on the basis of liking rather than wanting. Use the HEAL process to enrich and absorb the experience of this choice so that it becomes increasingly stable in you.

If a like becomes a want, step back from it and label it to yourself, such as: "Really wanting that beer." "So revved up about proving this point." "Spending too much time on this clothing website." Observe the wanting as a part of yourself that is off to the side or in the distance, perhaps imagining that it's like an amusingly insistent dog pulling you in the wrong direction. Take a few breaths to calm and center yourself. Disengage from any sense of pressure, compulsion, or "must-ness." Consciously let go of wanting. Recenter yourself in enjoyment and purposefulness—without wanting.

FEEL ALREADY SATISFIED

Any experience in which there is a sense of *satisfaction*—such as gratitude, pleasure, and accomplishment—is an opportunity to feel that this need has been met, at least for the moment. In addition to specific experiences, also be mindful of the general sense of being already full, that this moment is already enough; try the practice in the box. If you repeatedly internalize these experiences of satisfaction—even mild and passing experiences in daily life—they will gradually build up an unconditional feeling of contentment deep down inside you. Then you'll carry an underlying happiness with you wherever you go. You won't get so stressed about chasing pleasures or achievements. If they come, fine, and if not, well, you're already happy.

FEELING ALREADY FULL

Take a few breaths and relax. Notice that you are breathing ... that your heart is beating ... that you are going on living. There may be pain, illness, or disability, and there may be sorrow and suffering ... and meanwhile you can focus on what *is* sufficient, on what *is* functioning. It could be good to have more ... and still there is an enoughness already. Let the sense of this enoughness sink in.

Recognize the nurturing fullness of the natural world, including its offering of oxygen to breathe and food to eat. No matter what might be missing in your life, there is still the abundance of nature, so many kinds of living things enabling you to live. Let yourself feel supported, protected, and fed by the fullness of life.

Consider the fullness of the material universe ... your body consisting of countless atoms, already present, already made, nothing you need to do to create them ... the fabric of matter and energy, space and time, from which you are woven already. Rest in this fullness, not needing to understand it, simply receiving it.

Be mindful of so much appearing in awareness in each moment ... so many sounds, sensations, images, emotions, and thoughts. Relax and recognize the almost overwhelming inherent fullness of ordinary experience itself. Allow the sense of this fullness to fill you.

Recognize that it's all right that experiences keep passing away, since they are continually replaced by new experiences. Let yourself feel filled by whatever arises in awareness even as it passes away. Already so full, let go of wanting anything more.

HEALTHY PASSION

As I said in the previous chapter, the sympathetic and parasympathetic branches of the nervous system work together like the gas and brake pedals of a car. The sympathetic nervous system activates during the fight-or-flight stress response, but it's also engaged when we're pursuing opportunities with enthusiasm, being assertive, making love, and cheering on children and friends. We need the sympathetic nervous system for healthy passion.

Just because there is a stressor—from a holiday dinner at your home to a high-stakes opportunity at work—doesn't mean you need to feel stressed. The activation of the sympathetic nervous system (SNS) is not inherently stressful. The key difference is whether positive or negative emotion is also present. To put it simply:

- SNS + positive emotion = healthy passion

- SNS + negative emotion = unhealthy stress

Positive Emotions and the Green Zone

To understand the relationship between emotions and stress, think about two examples from your own life. First, recall a time you pursued a big goal and there was a lot of stress involved. For instance, you might have been moving to a new city or taking on a major project. Remember some of the negative emotions you had—such as anxiety, frustration, and anger—and consider how these made you feel more stressed. Second, recall a time you went after a big goal while experiencing many positive emotions. Look back and see how these feelings lowered your stress.

Positive emotions keep you in the green zone as you become more active, intense, or passionate. Because the sympathetic nervous system evolved to help our ancestors fight or flee, it's easy for excitement to turn quickly into frustration or anger. For example, I remember watching the San Francisco 49ers on TV and whooping happily as they scored a touchdown, and then being flooded with irritation when my wife asked a simple question from another room. Sympathetic nervous system activation is like zooming down the highway. Going fast, you can cover more ground, but the smallest thing could make you crash. Positive emotions help you stay inside the guardrails.

Finding the Sweet Spot

There's a sweet spot where what you're doing is challenging enough to be engaging but not so challenging as to feel overwhelming. To find and stay in that sweet spot, try these approaches.

BE COMFORTABLE WITH YOUR BODY REVVING UP

If you are facing a challenge and start to feel tense or nervous, tell yourself that it is OK to speed up, breathe faster, and feel a rush of adrenaline. When you interpret things in this way—as your body's healthy way of coping—they can feel less stressful. Remember that you have handled similar challenges in the past, and see how you are handling the current situation effectively. This will help you be more confident and less stressed.

PRIME YOURSELF WITH POSITIVE EMOTION

Before entering a situation that could be exciting, intense, or even a little nerve-racking, lay a foundation of positive emotion. Bring to mind good feelings and attitudes that are *matched* to the basic need that is at stake. This is an application of the methods in the "Grow the Strengths You Need Most" section in Chapter 3. For example, if you are going to be running a meeting, call up past experiences in which your leadership was successful or your expertise was appreciated. Doing this will prime you to respond to any challenges with grace and good humor rather than tension and irritability.

WHEN YOU SPEED UP, WATCH OUT FOR NEGATIVE EMOTIONS

When you do hurry, get excited, or feel intense, keep a sharp lookout for negative emotions such as frustration or anger. It's like driving a race car under a yellow flag: keep going, but be careful.

If negative feelings come up, label them to yourself, such as "irritation," "worrying," "resentment." This will increase regulation by your prefrontal cortex and calm down your amygdala. Try to slow things down; pause a little longer than usual before you speak. Mentally, and perhaps physically, step back from the situation until the needle of your stress-o-meter climbs down from red to orange to yellow . . . to green again.

ENJOY THE JOURNEY

As you pursue a goal, look for signs of progress. Mark the small victories and notice the little accomplishments. This drip-drip-drip of mild experiences of success will be rewarding to your brain and help you stay in the sweet spot of healthy passion. For example, if my email inbox has fifty new messages, I try to feel a sense of completion as I deal with each one of them. Then the whole inbox doesn't seem so daunting.

INCLINING YOUR MIND

Most of us have at least a few things that we know would be good to do but it's hard to do them. Similarly, there are a few things that would be good to stop doing, but we keep doing them. For example, I know I should exercise more and eat fewer carbohydrates.

Even when we're moving toward the right goals, sometimes we go about it in the wrong ways. Our deepest aims are always positive, since they're grounded in our basic needs for safety, satisfaction, and connection. For example, beneath desires to eat a bag of cookies are deep aims for comfort and satisfaction; under desires to impress others are deep aims for self-worth and connection. Most of the trouble we get into is about not our deepest aims but *how* we go about achieving them. Consider a desire that's been troubling for you, perhaps for certain foods or experiences, and ask yourself: "What's the deep aim at the bottom of it?" And when you get the answer, ask yourself: "How could I pursue this aim in better ways?"

When you're trying to motivate yourself toward a particular goal or to pursue that goal in wiser ways, it's important to take practical actions to set yourself up to succeed. For example, arrange for a walking buddy to meet you each morning to get more exercise, or clear the candy out of the cupboard if you'd like to eat fewer sweets. It's useful to do these things. But most of us already know the practical actions that would set us on the path—and we're still not walking it. So, how do we get ourselves to head in the right direction and away from the wrong one?

THE MOTIVATIONAL CIRCUIT

This is where a little knowledge about a key motivational circuit in your brain can be very useful. As the sense of reward in an experience increases, neurons in the *ventral tegmental area* at the top of your brain stem release more dopamine in two other regions in your brain: the nucleus accumbens inside the subcortex and the prefrontal cortex behind your forehead. In the nucleus accumbens, a spike of dopamine activity sends signals through the *globus pallidus* and *thalamus* that prompt you to take action toward the rewards. In the prefrontal cortex, increased dopamine activity focuses attention on what is rewarding. It also stimulates prefrontal *executive functions* to figure out how to keep the rewards coming and get even more of them. The ventral tegmental area, nucleus accumbens, and prefrontal cortex form a kind of circuit that also operates when we see opportunities and *potential* rewards.

To put this circuit to work for you, it helps to strengthen the association in your brain between the actions you'd like to encourage and the rewards that will come from them. I'll show you how to do this a little later in this chapter. You can also use this method to develop new ways of acting to replace old ways that you'd like to discourage. For instance, to help yourself not get heated with a provocative relative or co-worker, keep focusing on what feels rewarding in staying calm and centered. You'll be *extinguishing* a bad habit while *reinforcing* a good one.

Temperamental Differences

As you strengthen the association between certain behaviors and their rewards, take your temperament into account. Different people have different quantities of *dopamine receptors* inside the motivational circuit. Neurons connect with each other at tiny gaps called *synapses*. When a neuron fires, it releases neurotransmitters that move across this gap toward the receptors of other neurons. Receptors are like docking stations and neurotransmitter molecules are like little ships.

They land very quickly because the space between neurons is so small that several thousand synapses could fit inside the width of a single hair.

When neurotransmitters bond to receptors, that affects whether the receiving neuron will fire or not. Neurons with fewer dopamine receptors need more incoming dopamine to trigger dopamine-related activity. To simplify, *the fewer dopamine receptors that a person has, the more rewards that person needs to stay motivated.* Some people find it easy to stay on task and keep plugging away even if it's not very rewarding; these people tend to have more dopamine receptors. Other people lose interest pretty quickly if something is not stimulating or otherwise rewarding; they tend to have fewer receptors. These are normal variations, one aspect of natural temperamental diversity. My guess is that as our ancestors evolved, it was useful to have a variety of temperaments in their small bands. Individuals with fewer dopamine receptors, for example, could contribute to the band by looking for new opportunities, ideas, and ways of doing things.

It is not a character flaw to have relatively few dopamine receptors. It just means that a person is aided by increasing three things: the *amount* of reward, the *attention* on it, and the *sensitivity* to it. In fact, increasing these three things will help anyone to keep inclining the brain, and therefore the mind, in a positive direction.

You can increase the amount of reward in several ways:

- Choose activities that are more stimulating and pleasurable (e.g., get exercise through playing a sport rather than jogging on a treadmill).

- Add new rewards, such as doing an activity with other people.

- Vary the details of what you're doing. For example, if you're shifting your diet toward healthier meals, keep trying new recipes.

- Take frequent short breaks, and then come back to the task.

- Ask for frequent feedback, especially positive.

Highlight Rewards

In addition to creating new rewards, you can highlight the rewards that are already present by putting more attention on them and becoming more sensitive to them. This is worth doing in its own right, and sometimes it's not possible to create new rewards.

BEFORE DOING IT

Pick something that you are trying to motivate in yourself. See yourself doing it, and at the same time imagine what would be enjoyable or important about it. For example, to get myself to use my treadmill and grind uphill for half an hour, I'll imagine how good it will feel to have a break and listen to music and read something while chugging along. You can also imagine the rewards that will come in the future, after you have done the activity.

When you anticipate rewards in this way, move from the idea of the reward to an emotional and embodied sense of it, which will release more dopamine. Using my treadmill example, I try to bring to mind the pleasurable relaxed *feeling* I have when listening to my favorite playlist. This is a lot more motivating than just knowing intellectually that there will be music. If you've used the HEAL steps in the past to install the feeling of a beneficial experience, such as listening to music, then it will be easier to evoke this feeling in the present—like storing good experiences in a kind of bank that you can draw upon later.

WHILE DOING IT

When you are doing whatever it is that you want to motivate, repeatedly focus on what feels pleasurable about it. Again and again and again: this is how to create surges of dopamine that will train the motivational circuit.

Keep looking for what could be fresh or surprising about what you're doing. Dopamine spikes when the brain encounters novelty. Also, help yourself get as excited or intense as is appropriate. This increases adrenaline, which strengthens the association between the activity and its rewards.

AFTER DOING IT

When you are done, take a little time to savor the results. Getting off the treadmill, I focus on feelings of vitality and satisfaction that I did something for my health. Don't shift into the next thing without registering the rewards of what you have just done. You worked for them and deserve them.

Encourage Yourself

I've gone rock climbing with guides and most of them have been very encouraging. They told me when I made a mistake, but they emphasized how I was making progress. They brought out the best in me as a climber and made me want to keep climbing. On the other hand, one fellow was very different. He climbed ahead and yanked at the rope when I slowed down at the harder sections. He pointed out all my errors of technique but only watched impassively as I moved smoothly through a tricky traverse. His impatience and exasperation traveled down the rope like an angry scolding. Instead of making me improve, it made me self-conscious, worried, and stressed. It made me climb worse. He was an excellent climber but a poor guide.

Much the same thing happens inside a person's mind. There are basically two ways to get yourself up the mountains of life: through guidance or criticism, through drawing on the inner nurturer or the inner critic. Consider the differences between these two approaches:

GUIDANCE	CRITICISM
What is the goal	What isn't the goal
What's right	What's wrong
Kind tone	Harsh tone
Compassionate	Dismissive
Builds up	Tears down

As you pursue your goals, notice what it feels like to guide yourself and what it feels like to criticize yourself. Deliberately emphasize the attitude and feeling of guidance. Bring to mind people who are supportive and encouraging, and imagine how they would talk to you after you have made a mistake. Cheer yourself on. Repeatedly use the HEAL steps to take in experiences of self-guidance so it becomes increasingly natural for you.

Many people fear that if they're not hard on themselves, they'll just goof off, but this doesn't have to be true. Try to recognize repeatedly that you can keep yourself on the high road through guidance rather than criticism. Also recognize that being critical of yourself *lowers* performance over time. For example, the stress of beating yourself up over what you did wrong releases cortisol, which gradually weakens your hippocampus and consequently your brain's capacity to learn from what you did right.

If you know your course is good, even if it is not immediately rewarding, stay with it. This is the essence of motivation: being able to sustain action based on knowing in the core of your being that you should do something. I once took a class on meditation from Joseph Goldstein, a precise and no-nonsense teacher. At a break, I told him what I was experiencing and asked if I was on the right track. He nodded and then smiled and said two words I've never forgotten: "Keep going."

KEY POINTS

- Resilience is more than bouncing back from adversity. People who are resilient keep pursuing their goals in the face of challenges. Consequently, learning how to regulate your brain's motivational machinery is a key aspect of resilience.

- Liking is distinct from wanting. Wanting comes with a sense of insistence, drivenness, or compulsion that is stressful and can lead to harmful behaviors. Explore the experience of liking something without wanting it. Repeatedly take in experiences of being already satisfied to build up a core of contentment. Then you can enjoy pleasures and be ambitious without the stress of wanting.

- The sympathetic nervous system brings energy and passion. But without positive emotions such as happiness and love, sympathetic activation draws us into red zone stress. When you speed up, watch out for negative emotions, and keep looking for ways to experience positive ones.

- The brain has a fundamental motivational circuit based on dopamine activity. There are natural variations in the quantity of dopamine receptors that individuals have. People with fewer receptors tend to need more rewards to stay motivated.

- Train this circuit by increasing the association between rewards and whatever you'd like to motivate yourself toward. Increase the amount of rewards, your attention on them, and your sensitivity to them.

- People often think they need to be hard on themselves to stay motivated, but the opposite is generally true. Use guidance rather than criticism to stay on your course.

CHAPTER 9

INTIMACY

*I would rather walk with a friend in
the dark, than alone in the light.*

—Helen Keller

I was isolated and withdrawn as a child, and much of the time it felt like I was observing people from a great distance, as if I were on the outside of a restaurant window looking in, watching people talking and laughing together. I could see but not touch, hear but not speak. It took me a long time to get up the nerve to come in from the cold. I gradually opened up, slowly but surely knowing and being known by others, and becoming increasingly connected with them. Broadly speaking, this is *intimacy*, whose root meaning is "to make familiar or known."

There are degrees of intimacy in all our relationships, from a passing encounter with a hot dog vendor to a marriage of fifty years. Intimacy rests on a foundation of personal autonomy, empathy, compassion and kindness, and unilateral virtue in relationships. These are the topics of this chapter, in which I'll emphasize ways to work with your mind. In the next chapter, we'll focus on ways to interact with others.

ME AND WE

The greater the intimacy, the greater the rewards—and the greater the risks. As you open up and invest in relationships, you inevitably become more exposed and vulnerable. Then others can more easily disappoint or hurt you. How can we gain the benefits of intimacy while managing the challenges that come with it?

Paradoxically, in order to get the most out of "we," you need to stay centered in "me." As the proverb puts it, fences make for good neighbors. A strong sense of autonomy—that you are your own person and make your own choices—fosters depth of intimacy. For example, when you feel grounded in your body, it's easier to stay open to the feelings of other people. When you take care of your needs, there's a natural receptivity to the needs of others. Knowing you can step back aids stepping in.

Much as autonomy enables intimacy, intimacy supports autonomy. Close and nurturing relationships help a person feel safe and worthy as an individual, which promotes a confident independence. In a positive cycle, autonomy and intimacy feed each other. Together, they make you more resilient.

The Effect of Personal History

When there is less autonomy—when a person feels overwhelmed, pushed around, or entangled with other people—there will be less intimacy, especially over time. But staying "me" when dealing with "we" can be hard to do. Ask yourself whether you're able to maintain a comfortable sense of autonomy when others do any of these things:

- Want things from you
- Are upset with you

- Try to persuade or influence you

- Don't respect your boundaries

- Attempt to dominate or control you

How a person reacts to challenges to autonomy depends in part on his or her temperament. There is normal variation in the priority that people place on autonomy compared to intimacy. These natural differences in sociability and extroversion/introversion can be seen in childhood, and they persist into adulthood. The joke about parents is that with your first child everything seems to be about "nurture," but after the second one you realize how much depends on "nature."

Still, "nurture"—what happens to you and what you do with it, starting with the first breath and continuing through the last—makes an enormous difference. Beginning at birth, you began to explore independence and individuality: choosing where you would look and what you would swallow or spit out; discovering that the warmth against your skin came from another body; learning that others could have thoughts and feelings different from yours. Along the way, you naturally made messes and mistakes and sometimes got on the nerves of others.

And then the world responded. Some parents, relatives, teachers, and cultures value and support a child's independence and individuality, and some do not, with a big range in between. Thousands of little episodes in which a child's self-expression and assertiveness are accepted and managed skillfully—or not—add up over time to shape a person one way or another.

Think about your history, and take some time to answer these questions, which focus on your experiences related to autonomy. In childhood, what did you observe *around* you, such as how your siblings or other children were treated when they were opinionated, upset, or stubborn? What happened *to* you if you acted this way? How did this affect you when you were young? Also think about your life so far as an adult, and how others have treated you. Has it felt safe to be your true self out loud? Have you needed to push down your needs to keep the peace? When you've been strong and assertive, have others been reasonably receptive—or not?

Growing Autonomy

Then step back and ask yourself how this history might be affecting you today. It's normal to internalize how others treated you— such as limiting, suppressing, or shaming your individuality and independence—and then do that to yourself. In important relationships, consider how comfortable you are with:

- Fully expressing your thoughts and feelings

- Asking for what you want

- Trusting your judgment if others disagree with you

- Standing up to others

Wherever you start from, there are many effective ways to strengthen a healthy sense of "me" in the midst of "we."

FOCUS ON YOUR OWN EXPERIENCE

Notice if your attention is "pulled" into others and away from yourself. When this happens, return to your own experience, grounded in your body. What you are experiencing is not right or wrong, justified or unjustified. It simply is what it is, and you can stay centered in an ongoing awareness of it.

IMAGINE BOUNDARIES BETWEEN YOU AND OTHERS

Get a sense of other people being over *there* while you are separate and over *here*. You could imagine a line drawn on the ground between you and others, or a picket fence, or if need be an unbreakable wall of glass. Goofy as it is, I hear Captain Kirk's voice from *Star Trek* in my head: "Shields up, Scotty!"

INSIDE YOURSELF, ASSERT YOUR AUTONOMY

Recall times you felt determined and strong. Focus on the sense of this in your body. Deliberately tell yourself things such as: "I get to decide what's right for me." "I don't have to agree with you." "You and I are different and that's OK." "I do not have to give you what you want." For practical reasons, you may have to put up with some things—you might have to listen to a boss ramble in order to keep your job, or smile politely to an irritating relative at a family dinner to keep the peace. But know that you are making this choice yourself, doing the best you can according to your *own* values.

CALL ON INNER ALLIES

Intimacy supports autonomy, so tune into an internal sense of others who are on your side, which will help you stand up for yourself. Think about people who like you and who honor your independence. Imagine what they might say if others were being intense, pushy, or manipulative toward you. Bring to mind the feeling of the "caring committee" we explored in Chapter 6. Turn up the volume, as it were, of those who support you, and turn down the volume of those who are challenging your autonomy.

EMPATHY

Empathy is tuning into and understanding other people. When you feel grounded as "me," you're able to be empathic without getting flooded or overwhelmed.

Empathy is necessary for intimacy. It helps us make sense of tone and nuance, read intentions correctly, recognize the hurt under anger, and see the being behind the other person's eyes. Then we can communicate and interact more skillfully. At work and elsewhere, empathy bridges differences in a multicultural world. It helps us *feel felt*, in Dan Siegel's phrase. We live in and as individual bodies, each one mortal and often suffering. Empathy is the foundation of the sense that "I am not alone, others are with me, we are in this together, we share a common humanity."

Empathy does not mean approval or agreement. You can empathize with someone without waiving your rights and needs. In fact, empathy is very useful during conflicts, or in general with people you don't particularly like. Understanding them better could help you be more effective with them. And if they sense your empathy, they could feel more heard and become more willing to hear you.

Your Brain on Empathy

As hominids and humans evolved, they became more empathic. Today, in our very social brain, empathy is enabled by three neural systems that tune into the thoughts, emotions, and actions of others:

- **Thoughts.** Behind your forehead, the *prefrontal cortex* enables you to understand another person's beliefs, values, and plans.

- **Emotions.** On the inside of the temporal lobes on the sides of your head, the *insula* gets engaged when you sense the feelings of others.

- **Actions.** In different parts of your brain, *mirror-like networks* activate both when you do something—such as reaching for a cup—and when you see another person doing it.

In a very efficient way, these regions in your brain do double duty. They regulate your own thoughts, emotions, and actions while at the same time helping you to understand, from the inside out, those of others.

Growing Empathy Inside Yourself

People tend to think that empathy is just there—you have it or you don't. But you can develop greater empathy, much like growing any other psychological resource. Let's start by exploring some good ways to do this, and then see how to tap into empathy when you're interacting with others.

GO DEEP INTO YOUR INTERIOR

Increasing self-awareness—especially of the deepest layers of your experience—improves other-awareness. So tune into the nuances of sensations, emotions, thoughts, and desires inside yourself. In particular, sense down into the softer and often younger material beneath the surface of your stream of consciousness. It's like seeing a leaf floating down a river: reaching for it, you find that it's connected to a twig, and then a branch, and then a very interesting log. Also try to track rapid changes in the flow of your experience. In your brain, neurons are routinely firing five to fifty times a second, so a lot can happen over the course of a single breath. With practice, you will increase your granularity of mindfulness.

STEP OUT OF YOUR PERSPECTIVE

To become more empathic, it helps to become more comfortable with casting loose from the familiar moorings of your beliefs and judgments to enter another person's inner world. Explore what it's like to hold your views and values lightly, and to appreciate that things that seem self-evident and important to you often do not seem that way to others. Recognize the powerful impact of life experiences on other people, including the effects of their parents, culture, wounds, and stresses. Much as it's made sense for you to become who you are because of your background, what others have become because of their background makes sense as well. Pick a charged topic in a significant relationship—such as how housework should be shared—and imagine how you would approach it if you had the beliefs, values, and background of the other person.

INCREASE YOUR "CULTURAL COMPETENCE"

This means becoming more knowledgeable about and skillful with people who belong to a group that's different from your own. As a white, male, cisgender, heterosexual, American, middle-class, able-bodied, professional person, I have found it extremely useful (and, I think, moral) to learn more about people who are not like me. It's made me more aware of my own unconscious assumptions and biases, and more respectful of others' priorities and ways of acting. Cultural competence gives us insight into how we interpret what others say or do, and insight into how others could interpret our own words and actions. A greater understanding of different types of people helps us have more empathy for our effects on them.

Tapping into Empathy While Interacting

In routine situations or with familiar people, it's easy to go on autopilot and let empathy fade into the background. And if others are critical or blaming, empathy tends to fly out the window. When we really need it, empathy can seem most out of reach. So it's good to develop a deliberate habit of empathic understanding when you're with other people.

PAY ATTENTION

It usually takes a conscious effort to sustain attention, especially when the other person has thoughts, feelings, or desires that are different from or at odds with yours. Consider how rare it is for other people to stay present and attentive to you for several minutes in a row—and how good it feels when they do. Imagine a little monitor inside your mind that pays attention to how well you are paying attention. In your brain, this involves a region called the *anterior cingulate cortex*. If your mind wanders a bit, that's natural. Just bring it back.

STAY OPEN

Relax your body, especially in the area of your chest and heart. Be aware of any tension, bracing, or guarding, and see if you can let go of it. If you start to feel uncomfortable or flooded as you open to the other person, reestablish a strong sense of "me." You could imagine that you are deeply rooted like a sturdy tree, and that the thoughts and feelings of others are passing through you like wind through leaves. Remind yourself that you don't have to agree with or approve of anything if you don't want to, which will help you be more receptive toward other people.

TRACK MICRO-EXPRESSIONS AND MICRO-TONES

Look into the other person's eyes as much as is appropriate. Notice any discomfort you may feel with eye contact. Don't be invasive, but also be willing to extend the contact for a second or a breath longer than you normally would. It's a profound way to receive another person.

Research by Paul Ekman and others has shown that underlying emotions and attitudes are often revealed by fleeting facial expressions, especially around the eyes and mouth. Observe these, and also be aware of the other person's posture, as well as speed and intensity of movement. Imagine what you would be feeling and wanting if you had those facial expressions and that body language yourself. This will tend to engage the mirror-like networks in your brain that tune into the actions of others.

One of the recent developments in human evolution is the ability to produce and to hear rapid and subtle changes in tone of voice. The most recent branch of the *vagus nerve complex* extends up into the middle ear and face, and it is a key element of the *social engagement system* in your brain and body. Focusing attention on the vocal tones of other people will draw on the vagus nerve complex and deepen your empathy for them.

SENSE BENEATH THE SURFACE

Try to get a feeling for the deeper needs and pains in the other person. For example, there could be fear behind aggressiveness or desires for closeness underneath a pushing away. Imagine what the person's body feels like, and whether there is fatigue, illness, or pain. Try to have an intuitive sense of what might be going on deep down inside *you* if you were acting like the other person. Doing this will engage the insula inside your brain, increasing your empathy for the emotional life of other people.

REFINE YOUR UNDERSTANDING

A kind of thoughtful hypothesis-testing is a key element of empathy, and it draws on your prefrontal cortex. So develop specific though tentative ideas about what's going on with the other person. Next, test your ideas by looking for evidence for or against them. For example, consider what you know about the other person's temperament and personal history; maybe what you thought was a deliberate effort to hurt you in particular was mainly an automatic way of reacting to people in general that was acquired in that person's childhood. Then refine your ideas to have a more accurate empathic understanding.

WARMING THE HEART

With empathy, we can have a real sense of the sorrows and joys of others. But this sense is not itself compassion and kindness, which must be added to empathy for them to be present in the moment. And over time, we can develop greater compassion and kindness as personal traits. Truly, each of us can become a more loving individual.

Besides being good for other people, strengthening the (metaphorical) muscle of the heart calms your body, protects its immune system, lifts your mood, and evokes caring from others. Compassion presupposes suffering, while kindness does not; in practice, these two typically come as a blend, so I'll treat them together here. In the first chapter, we explored how to apply compassion and kindness to yourself. Now let's see how you can cultivate a warmer heart for others.

SAVOR WARMHEARTEDNESS

When you feel compassionate or kind, stay with the experience, mark it to yourself as important, open to it in your body, and sense that it is sinking into you and becoming a part of you. Try to do this at least a few times a day, for a few moments or longer. Additionally, set aside some time for a sustained practice of compassion and kindness, such as the one in the box.

COMPASSION AND KINDNESS

Settle into yourself and relax. Bring to mind someone who has helped you, such as a parent or teacher. Be aware of this person's challenges, stress, and pain. Find a tenderhearted concern, perhaps with soft thoughts such as "May you not suffer . . . may this pain pass . . . may your health improve." Embody and intensify the experience with a hand on your heart. Then shift from compassion to kindness, to wishing that the person be happy. Inside yourself, find a friendliness, perhaps lovingness. You could think: "May you be successful . . . may you be at peace . . . may you know you are loved."

Bring to mind your mate or a friend. Be aware of this person's burdens, disappointments, and suffering. Open to compassion, with warmth in your heart and supportive thoughts such as "May your job be less stressful . . . may the medical treatment go well." Also find a sense of kindness and affection. Know what compassion and kindness feel like in your body, and let them establish themselves inside you, sinking in and becoming a part of you.

Next, pick someone you feel neutral about. Imagine this person's losses, loneliness, and pain—and find compassion. Also find kindness and goodwill. You might think: "May you be healthy . . .

may you be safe . . . may you live with ease . . . may you be truly happy."

And then simply rest in a general sense of compassion and kindness, not focusing on any one person. Imagine waves of sweet concern, warmth, friendliness, and love rippling out from you. Sense that as you inhale, lovingness flows into you; as you exhale, lovingness flows out from you. Be aware of whatever is enjoyable, beautiful, or valuable in this experience. Give over to compassion and kindness, and let these carry you along.

RECOGNIZE SUFFERING

Walk down any street and you'll see tiredness, strain, and sadness in the faces of others. Life contains many things besides suffering, but everyone suffers at least some of the time. Nonetheless, in our routines and busyness, it's easy to tune this out and move right past it. One time I asked a teacher of mine, Gil Fronsdal, what he focused on in his own life. He was quiet for a moment and then he said, "I stop for suffering."

As you interact with others at home or work, open to the suffering that could be there, such as quiet disappointment and dismay. A few times a day, look at a stranger or distant acquaintance and get a feeling for the burdens that person is carrying. This opens and softens the heart.

SEE OUR COMMON HUMANITY

In general, we're more inclined to be compassionate and kind toward people we think are like us in some way. Try to look for commonalities with others—particularly with those who seem very unlike you. For example, bring someone to mind and think: "Just like me, you feel pain . . . You get hurt and angry when people treat you badly . . . You worry about your children . . . Just like me, you want to be happy." See if you can get a sense of the person as once a child like you. At the bottom of beliefs or ways of life that seem very different from yours, try to find longings and feelings that are like your own.

SEPARATE APPROVAL FROM COMPASSION

Moral judgment is separate from compassion. We can have compassion for suffering itself even when it's occurring in people who are the source of their own suffering or who have harmed others. If there was compassion only for the people we liked, the world would be a much colder and crueler place.

Think about someone who is hard to feel compassion for. Be aware of your criticism, frustration, or anger about that person. Imagine all that placed on one side of a line. And then distinct from all that, on the other side of the line, can you find the wish that *all* beings not suffer—including people who have trespassed upon you or contributed to their own troubles? Separate your analysis and judgments from a simple compassion for suffering, any suffering. Acknowledge what's true about the other person . . . and then find compassion. Besides the moral value of doing this, it will help you feel freer and more at peace with that person.

COMPASSION FOR A DIFFICULT PERSON

Relax and center yourself. Bring to mind the feeling of being cared about. Get a sense of others being on your side. Feel a core of strength and determination inside yourself.

Think about someone who is difficult for you. Acknowledge to yourself what has been challenging, and how it's affected you, and what you plan to do about it. Then focus on the suffering of the person. You may need to look for an underlying strain, tension, or unhappiness—perhaps reaching back to childhood. But there is pain in everyone. And you can have compassion for it. If it helps, imagine how this person might act if there were less suffering inside.

Understandably, you could want this person to treat you or others differently. You may want an apology, compensation, or justice. Alongside all that, you can also wish that this person not be in needless pain, not be miserable, and not have misfortune land on people that he or she loves.

Get a sense of your basic decency and your desire to relieve the suffering of others. See if you can genuinely think this about the other person: "May you not suffer." Try to find other words as well, such as: "I do not want to add to your pain . . . deep down, may you be at peace."

As you find compassion toward this person, you may feel less challenged or upset. Know that whatever this person has done cannot alter the fundamental goodness deep inside your own heart.

UNILATERAL VIRTUE

As a longtime couples therapist, I've watched a kind of movie unfold in my office many times. The details change along with the actors, but the basic script is the same:

Person A: I'm hurt and angry and want you to treat me better.
Person B: I'm hurt and angry, too, and I want you to treat *me* better.
Person A: Well, I'll treat you better if *you* treat me better.
Person B: OK, I'll do it—but you go first!

Whether at home or at work, it's easy to spend more time dwelling on the faults of others than reflecting on the room for improvement in oneself. But waiting for others to change first creates deadlocks, vicious cycles, and a sense of helplessness. Meanwhile, people marinate in hurt, resentment, and grudges—which get prioritized for storage by the brain because of its negativity bias.

The alternative is *unilateral virtue*, in which you draw on autonomy, empathy, compassion, and kindness to be honorable and responsible even when others aren't. This approach to relationships simplifies things. Instead of getting lost in what others ought to be doing, you focus on your own actions. This approach also supports a sense of agency by emphasizing where you *do* have influence, which is mainly over yourself, not others. Unilateral virtue feels good in its own right, pulls your attention away from negative preoccupations about other people, and helps you feel the "bliss of blamelessness" as you know that you've been doing everything you can.

Unilateral virtue is not about knuckling under to anyone or being a doormat. You still have compassion for yourself, speak up for your needs, and observe what the other person does over time. This is your best-odds strategy for encouraging others to treat you well. As you address what they want and step out of repetitive quarrels, people usually become more receptive and reasonable. And having taken care of your side of the street, you're in a stronger position to ask them to take care of theirs.

Know Your Own Code

Unilateral virtue starts with knowing how you truly want to speak and act. This is your personal "code of conduct." While it might be influenced by others, fundamentally it's up to you to decide what's on it.

Pick a messy, difficult relationship. In your mind or on paper, make some notes about the dos and don'ts that you'd like to follow. These could be moral standards, skillful approaches, and agreements you've made. For example, I've had these in some of my challenging relationships:

DO	DON'T
Remember they've had a hard day	Interrupt
Start by saying what I agree with	Lose my temper
Call if I'm going to be late	Hassle people
Leave early and arrive on time	Get caught up in proving my point
Admit my own part of the problem	Argue about the past
Try to anticipate their needs	Be over-critical

Take a few minutes to imagine how things might go if you operated according to this code, especially during conflicts. It's not a guarantee of improved results, but it increases their likelihood. And no matter what the other person does, in your heart you'll know you did what you could. Having a clear code may seem so obvious that it's easy to ignore, but knowing what's in it—it's particularly helpful to write it down—is very useful, especially in difficult relationships.

Live Unilaterally

If you fall short of your code sometimes, that's normal. I fall short myself. That doesn't mean giving up. Occasionally it means double-checking that your code is realistic and that what's in it truly matters to you. If appropriate, revise it and commit to the updated version. But usually it just means noticing that you need to return to the high road. Here are some suggestions for staying on that path, especially with those who are most challenging for you.

FILL YOUR OWN CUP

When you take care of your own needs, you naturally become more patient and generous with others. No matter how good your intentions, you can't pour milk out of an empty carton. Think about what we've explored about being on your own side, enjoying life, and taking care of your body. It's much easier to stay out of the red zone when you are rested, well nourished, and happy.

CLEAR WHAT CLOUDS YOUR REACTIONS

Consider times when it's been hard to act with unilateral virtue, and ask yourself: what were the contributing factors? Perhaps it was lack of food or sleep, too much alcohol, or already being irritated by a stressful day at work. Perhaps your grievances with the other person turbocharged your reactions. Consider how previous life experiences—particularly in childhood—might have affected you. Whatever the factors are, be aware of them, and if they are in play— such as discussing a charged topic with your partner after you've had a glass of wine—be extra careful.

STAY FOCUSED

At home or on the job, when you have been doing your share of the work while also being careful with your words and tone, it can be so tempting to comment critically on those who have not. Maybe the comment takes the form of a nonverbal eye roll or exasperated sniff, but it's still there. If you do need to address something with someone, we'll explore how to do this in the next chapter. But usually these comments just leak out as the worst of both worlds: not clear and serious enough to get your needs met, yet provocative and inflammatory enough to trigger a quarrel. Instead, it's better to focus on your own responsibilities and staying true to your code.

ADDRESS THEIR REQUESTS AND COMPLAINTS

In some families and cultures, it's almost taboo to ask for something or say what's bothering you. But since we depend on each other, we must ask things of each other. And when people feel let down or mistreated, they need to be able to speak up—to "complain" in the simple sense of the word.

Recall a time when someone responded to one of your requests or complaints. How did that feel? How did it help the relationship? You provide similar benefits to the other person and to the relationship as a whole when you do this yourself.

Most of the time, the requests and complaints of others boil down to relatively small and doable thoughts, words, or deeds: "Can you remember our anniversary?" "I get really upset when you yell at me." "Can you put the cap back on the toothpaste?" "I need you to give me your full attention when we're talking." Delivering the goods to the other person may have costs to you of time and attention, but these are usually much less than the costs of tension and conflict. Plus you gain the benefits of what the other person would be more willing to deliver to you in return.

People are rarely perfect communicators, and their requests and complaints often come wrapped in euphemisms, confusing word clouds, exaggerations, side issues, falsehoods, moralizing, accusations, excuses for their own bad behavior, demands, and threats. Remember that you don't have to agree with or get distracted by the stack of hay surrounding the one actual needle you intend to address. Do your best to find the needle, decide for yourself what you can reasonably do, and then consistently do it.

Think about how you'd feel toward other people who treated *you* in this way. When you act with unilateral virtue yourself—along with autonomy, empathy, compassion, and kindness—you'll be laying the foundation for healthy, cooperative, and fulfilling relationships.

KEY POINTS

- Degrees of intimacy are present in all relationships, not just romantic ones.

- A strong "me" in the midst of "we" fosters intimacy. This sense of personal autonomy is supported by establishing good boundaries and asserting your individuality inside your mind.

- Empathy is necessary for intimacy. In the brain, different neural networks help us to tune into the thoughts, emotions, and actions of others. You can develop more empathy inside yourself, and you can tap more of that empathy when you interact with others.

- Compassion and kindness can be strengthened inside you like any other psychological resource. Recognize suffering, see our common humanity, separate approval from compassion, and deliberately internalize warmhearted caring toward others.

- Focusing on the faults of others creates deadlocks and resentment. It's better to practice unilateral virtue: focusing on your own responsibilities and personal code of conduct no matter what others do. This brings the "bliss of blamelessness," reduces conflicts, and increases the odds that others will treat you well.

PART FOUR

RELATING

CHAPTER 10

COURAGE

One is wise who is peaceable,
friendly, and fearless.

—The Dhammapada

I've had some seriously scary moments high in the mountains. But most of the times that I've felt anxious have been around other people. I think this is true for most of us. We need courage in our relationships, and the root meaning of this word is very appropriate: "heart."

In this chapter, we'll see how to protect and stand up for yourself so that you both are safe and *feel* safe with other people. We'll start with how to speak from the heart with self-respect and skill. Then we'll explore effective ways to assert yourself, and finish with how to make repairs in a relationship.

SPEAKING FROM THE HEART

Think about a significant relationship. It could be with a mate, child, sibling, parent, friend, or co-worker. If you've felt let down, irritated, or hurt, have you been able to talk about it? If you appreciate or love this person, have you expressed it? If you've been at fault sometimes, have you admitted it?

When important things are left unsaid, it leads to resentment, loneliness, and lost opportunities to discover your truth by speaking it. People in a relationship often don't say what they could about what's felt good and what's felt bad and what they really wish would be different. They're like two boats floating near each other, and each undelivered communication drops between them like a heavy stone, with its waves pushing them farther apart.

Take a moment to think about the weight of what's been unsaid in your relationships. What have the effects been on you and other people?

Sometimes it's just not possible, appropriate, or safe to talk about something with another person. Then we need to draw on internal resources such as self-compassion. When it is in fact possible, it often feels scary to open up fully. It also takes skill to talk about hard things without making them worse. At these times we need *interpersonal courage* to stay safe and speak wisely with an open heart.

Safety First

Communicating authentically can have risks, such as emotional vulnerability and putting topics on the table that might upset a relationship. Here are some ways to keep it as safe as possible.

RECOGNIZE DANGER

It's a sad reality that violence or the threat of it shadows many relationships. If there is any risk of this, tell someone who could help you, such as a doctor, minister, or therapist. There are also many hotlines, shelters, and related resources. No one should have to worry about physical aggression in a relationship. As difficult as it may be, it is important to deal with this issue first, before bringing up anything else.

A different sort of danger is your words being used against you. For example, there might be lasting consequences for child custody after a divorce. Watch out for an innocence or hopefulness in yourself that, sweet as it is, could lead you into trusting another person more than is appropriate. After reflecting, you may still decide that you want to say something, but know what you could be getting into.

Also consider the danger of just upsetting a fragile person with no good result. For example, toward the end of their lives, there were things I hadn't told my mother and father, but saying my bit would have only troubled them.

KNOW YOUR TRUTH

Try to be very clear about what it is that you see, feel, and want in a particular relationship. Take some time to sort things out for yourself. Imagine saying everything in your heart to a friend or perhaps a spiritual being. You could write a letter you'll never send. If appropriate, talk about the relationship with someone else to unpack what's been happening and to consider what to do about it.

TALK ABOUT TALKING

Good conversations about important issues often zig and zag, get heated and then cool down, and eventually find a soft landing. It's OK if they're messy and don't follow some perfect script. But if it feels unsafe to bring up certain topics, or if interactions go off the rails or don't seem to be productive, then it could help to talk about talking. If the other person is not willing to discuss how you interact, that's a serious concern in any significant relationship. Good relationships are based on good interactions, and it's hard for a relationship to improve if its interactions don't.

As you get ready to talk about talking, think about what helps your interactions go well with the other person, and what makes them go badly. Then, when you do speak with each other, try to focus on dos and don'ts that apply to *both* of you and *from now on*. This way you're less likely to get sidetracked into blaming each other and arguing about the past. For example, you could try to agree to:

Give each other about the same amount of time to talk
Not bring up big issues right before bed
Not yell or make threats
Not argue in front of the children

Check that the words you're using are clear to each of you, such as what is "yelling" or "arguing." You could add a time-out rule, in which either of you can say you need a break for a minute or even the rest of the night—as long as you are willing to resume the conversation the next day.

Be careful to abide by the ground rules yourself. If the other person strays from them, try to discuss that and get back on track. Ultimately, disengage if you need to. I've been in situations in which I said essentially, "I do want to talk with you, but if you keep speaking to me in that way I'm going to have to leave."

You can't make other people treat you in a certain way, but you *can* say what you want. After that, you'll see what they do. Then you can decide for yourself what that means and what you intend to do about the relationship. For example, you might decide to steer clear of certain topics that just provoke an argument. Or step back from a relationship altogether.

Sharing Experiences and Solving Problems

Much communicating is simply sharing experiences: "I liked your presentation at the meeting." "I'm hungry." "It makes me mad when people assume I'll do all the dishes." "Isn't this sunset beautiful?" "I'm worried about our son." Another kind of communicating is about solving problems, in which people say things like: "This is my plan for the new product." "Please call the pediatrician." "I wish you would back me up in staff meetings." "No, you haven't been getting home in time for a family dinner." "If you quit interrupting me, it'll be easier to listen to you."

Both ways of talking are important, and they weave together in many interactions. Still, they are quite different, as you can see here:

SHARING EXPERIENCES	SOLVING PROBLEMS
How this has landed on me	What we ought to do about it
"I feel"	"There is"
"I am"	"You are"
Personal, subjective	Impersonal, objective
Focus on process, relationship	Focus on outcomes, solutions
Joined	Detached
You're the expert	Others can disagree about facts or plans
Your truth for its own sake	Persuasion, influence, insistence

We do need to solve problems, which I'll focus on in the next section. But "problem talk" can easily slide into arguments, especially if the topic is charged or if there is a backlog of undelivered communications. On the other hand, "experience talk" rests on safer ground. If you say, "It *is* bad when X happens," another person could dispute that, but if you say, "I *feel* bad when X happens," it's harder for someone to say, "Oh no you don't!" Your experience is not *itself* a demand upon others, so simply sharing it is less likely to provoke a push back. When you speak from your experience, it's easier to ask others to do the same.

Sharing your experience is usually worth doing in its own right. Additionally, if problem-solving is getting tense or contentious, it's useful to shift into experience talk—perhaps about what you are experiencing during the interaction. If your conversation moves back and forth between the two types of communicating, sometimes it helps to name the transition explicitly. For example, if you think you're sharing your feelings and the other person starts trying to "fix" you, it's jarring even when well intended. Plus it can carry an implicit message, such as: "I know more than you." "I'm the teacher and you're the student." "I'm healthy and you're not." On the other hand, if you think you're just trying to solve a practical problem and the other person keeps talking about feelings, it can be frustrating. It's like one person is doing ballet and the other person is doing the tango. Try to agree—tacitly or explicitly—about what sort of conversation you're having, so you're both doing the same dance.

It's often best to start with experience talk, and then shift as needed into problem talk. When our kids were young, I found a little motto—"Start by joining"—that made me a better father and husband. Moving into an interaction with empathy, compassion, and kindness is a form of joining. Sharing experiences rather than offering analysis or advice also promotes joining. When we feel connected to other people, it's easier to solve problems together.

Speaking Wisely

Relationships are built from interactions, and interactions are built from communications that go back and forth like a volley in tennis. When it's your turn to "hit the ball," you have a range of options depending on what the other person just said. Some of these options are wiser than others.

Wisdom is a fancy word, but it boils down to the combination of skillfulness and goodness. When you speak, all you can do is aim for the high end of your range of options. Then the other person will say something in response, sending the conversational ball your mental way, and you'll have another chance to send it back as wisely as possible. This way of looking at interactions is an aspect of unilateral virtue: it emphasizes your own responsibility for what you say, and it brings the peace of mind that comes from knowing you've done the best you can. It's also enlightened self-interest to reduce side issues—such as your tone of voice or a poorly chosen word—that others can focus on to avoid dealing with what you're trying to talk about.

What does speaking wisely mean, concretely? Think of a relationship or a recent interaction that's been challenging for you—perhaps conversations turn into fights or chilly strained silences—and see how the suggestions below might help.

HAVE A MENTAL CHECKLIST FOR SPEECH THAT IS WISE

For me, it's been very useful to keep in mind this definition of wise speech from the Buddhist tradition:

1. **Well intended:** is aimed at helping, not hurting; is not based on ill will

2. **True:** everything need not be said, but whatever *is* said is accurate and honest

3. **Beneficial:** is enjoyable or useful to others, oneself, or both

4. **Timely:** comes when it is appropriate

5. **Not harsh:** what is said may be firm, passionate, or heated, but the tone and words are not mean, belittling, or abusive

There's a sixth standard to be followed if possible, with speech that is:

6. **Wanted:** be thoughtful about intruding upon others; nonetheless, speak up as you judge best

If an interaction is going fine, keep on going. But if it gets heated or awkward, make sure that your own speech is still wise. In particular, check that your speech isn't harsh. It's not *what* we say, but *how* we say it, that's often most hurtful or provocative to others. As you use wise speech, get a sense of what this way of communicating feels like in your body, including your facial expressions, tone of voice, gestures, and posture. Repeatedly take in this sense, enriching and absorbing it, so wise speech becomes increasingly embodied and automatic for you.

SPEAK FOR YOURSELF

It's a classic piece of advice to emphasize "I-statements" instead of "you-statements." If you are open and genuine, it encourages the other person to do the same. Be careful about telling people what they think, feel, or intend, such as: "You did that on purpose." "You want to undermine me on this team." "You don't care." "You're projecting your mother onto me." "You only think about yourself." Instead, focus on statements like: "When you did that I felt hurt." "I felt undermined by you." "I don't feel respected by you."

TRY NONVIOLENT COMMUNICATION

Nonviolent communication (NVC) is a structured way of speaking that was developed by Marshall Rosenberg. It has complexities that are well worth looking into, but the essence is simple: "When X happens I feel Y because I need Z."

The first part, X, is described as factually as possible, like a neutral observer might. For example, you could say: *"When your report is incomplete . . ." "When you get home half an hour later than we agreed for dinner . . ." "When I'm talking and you don't look at me . . ." "When you almost never initiate sex . . ." "When you don't back me up when your father tells me how to be a better parent . . ."* But you would not say: *"When you drop the ball at work . . ." "When you don't care about this family . . ." "When your mind is wandering all over the place . . ." "When you don't like me . . ." "When you undermine me to keep your father happy . . ."*

The second part, Y, is about your experience, especially your emotions, sensations, and desires, instead of your opinions, judgments, or problem-solving. If we extend the examples of X just above, you might say: *"I feel worried about this project . . ." "I get angry and uncertain about whether you'll keep your promises . . ." "I feel lonely inside . . ." "I miss your affection . . ." "My whole body tightens up and I feel scared about our marriage . . ."* But you wouldn't say: *"I feel you're lazy and unreliable . . ." "I know you'd rather be at work . . ." "You're a bad listener . . ." "You don't want me . . ." "You think I'm a bad parent . . ."*

The third part, Z, names one or more universal, understandable human needs that underlie what you feel. Staying with the examples in X and Y, you could say: *"I need a sense of reliability with people at work." "Our kids need to know they're a priority for you." "I need to feel that I exist for other people." "I need to feel wanted as a lover, not just appreciated as a co-parent." "I need to feel that my partner is loyal to me."* But you would not say: *"I need you to wake up and take this job seriously." "Our kids don't need an absentee parent." "I need you to agree with me." "We must have sex twice a week." "You have to stop talking to your father."*

Lots of good conversations don't follow the exact forms of NVC. But if I'm talking with someone and it's getting heated or off track, I'll start using the NVC structure. Usually things go better when I do.

HOLD OTHERS IN YOUR HEART

In the heat of the moment, it's easy to get caught up in our own point of view and emotional roller coaster, and lose sight of what's happening inside other people. Maybe they're worried about their kids, frustrated with co-workers, or stressed about money. Their actions are influenced by many factors—a nagging headache, a late bus, the residues of childhood—that are not about you. You have to deal with the impacts of others upon you, but you may not need to take them so personally.

It's helpful to keep in mind the priorities and hot buttons of other people. For example, if they tend to be anxious, why set off needless alarms? If they react to certain words, you could try to make your point in other ways. If a friend was neglected or abandoned in childhood, understand why seemingly small things like arriving late for a lunch together could land hard. Some individuals place a lot of importance on autonomy, while different people care more about intimacy. If you emphasize one while someone else emphasizes the other, think about ways you could anticipate and address that person's priority while still being true to yourself.

In a sense, we all walk around with questions hanging over our heads like thought balloons, such as: "Do you respect me?" "Are you going to push me around?" "Do you see my pain?" "Are you for me or against me?" "Do you love me?" Relationships go better when we lead with authentic and reassuring answers to the questions in the minds of others. Often a simple word or look or touch is enough.

You may need to put someone out of your business affairs or circle of friends or even your bed. You may need to put someone out of your life altogether. But do you need to put this person out of your heart?

ASSERTING YOURSELF

In even the most supportive and positive relationships, we still need to assert ourselves, if only in small and subtle ways. This could look like making a persuasive case for a plan at work or asking explicitly for more help at home after your hints haven't gotten through. It may seem rude or pushy to be assertive, but it's natural for others to express themselves and try to get what they want, and it's natural for you to do the same. (From now on I'll use "want" in the general sense of "wish, aim, desire, or need"—usually perfectly appropriate—rather than in the narrow and problematic sense of "craving" used in Chapter 8.)

Relationships go smoothly when everyone wants the same things. But how common is that? For example, my mother and father wanted to watch different shows on our TV. They argued about this until they agreed that she'd get to pick on odd-numbered days and he'd take the even-numbered ones (trained as a scientist, he joked that this would give my mom seven extra days a year). Relationships also go well when everyone is doing their fair share. But again, is this always the case? If little comments and adjustments resolve issues like these, great. If not, here are skillful ways to address interpersonal issues.

Establish the Facts

Often the facts of a situation are not obvious, or people have different beliefs about them. Whatever the issue is, try to come to agreement about what the relevant facts are. That will usually narrow the issue and ground it in objective reality. For example, how often does someone arrive late for work? What loaded word was said in a fight? How much time is a teenager putting into homework? People can disagree about what facts *mean*, but facts themselves are just what's true.

On your own or with the other person, you could take a day or a week and observe what is truly happening. You may discover that what you were worried or irritated about is actually a rare or minor event. Or you may find even stronger evidence that helps you assert yourself more effectively.

Clarify the Values

Once facts are clear, they need to be related to *values*—which include priorities, principles, and preferences. For example, parents might agree that they rarely have dinners as a family, but disagree about how much that matters. People often think that the relevant values are obvious and shared by everyone—"Of course we should eat together" vs. "Of course we should not force our teenagers to eat with us"—when they're actually not.

Reflect on what is most important to you related to an issue, and *why* it is important. If you can, find out what the other person's values are. Try to get down to the deeper layers of temperament, upbringing, religious beliefs, and personal history that shape our values. See where the two of you care about things similarly, and where you just don't.

Then you have some options. You could:

- Explain how you feel or what you want in terms of the other person's values.

- Make a case for your own values.

- Create spheres of influence, in which your values govern what happens in one area (e.g., how reports are formatted at work, how much TV kids are allowed to watch) while the other person's values are applied in another area (e.g., how people talk in meetings, how hard kids need to work in school).

- Lighten up. If person A cares a lot about something while person B doesn't, maybe go with what A wants.

- Give up a value to fulfill other ones. For example, it could make sense to relax about having a tidy home for the sake of more fun time with your kids.

- Take a stand. If a value is important to you, you could decide you're going to push for it and let the chips fall where they may.

Keep Your Eyes on the Prize

Try to focus on the result you really care about, and don't chase other issues. For example, I did family therapy with a father who desperately wanted to feel more connected with his angry and withdrawn teenage son. The father would start out being relaxed and accepting, and I could see the son warming up to him. Then the dad would rush in with some well-intended but implicitly critical advice, and the boy would close up again. Over time, the father learned to stay with the good feelings of connection that were growing between him and his son. That was what he valued most, much more than giving advice.

Think about times when you're making a point and the other person throws a side issue or inflammatory comment at you. Then what do you do? Tempting as it is, it's usually best to let the pitch sail by without swinging at it, and simply return to your point. When I'm in these situations, in my mind I hear a line from an old *Star Wars* movie: "Stay on target! Stay on target!"

Consolidate Your Gains

Suppose you've been trying to make a friend understand why you felt hurt by something that happened between you, and finally it's clear. Maybe it's best to leave it at that, rather than bring up another problem in your relationship. Or suppose you're talking late at night with your spouse, who is slowly coming to realize that your child is indeed having trouble learning to read. It could be smart to wait until the morning to begin figuring out—and potentially disagreeing about—how to talk with the school.

You're unlikely to resolve a large issue in a single conversation, and the other person could start to feel pushed on if you pursue one issue after another. So it's often best to stop when you're ahead and protect whatever's been accomplished, such as a deeper emotional understanding of each other or a clear agreement about certain actions in the future. Then when the time is right, you can take the next step.

Focus on the Future

My mother had a huge heart. One way she expressed her love was by giving advice. When our children were little, she gave my wife and me a lot of advice about how to raise them, and after a while, it got on our nerves. So I asked my mom if, in the future, she could not give advice unless we asked for it. She said, "Oh, I don't do that!"

Right there I could have gotten into one of our typical arguments about the past. Instead, for once I had my wits about me and just muttered, "OK, then I guess it won't be a problem," and left it at that. Over the next day I could see my mom starting to tell us how to parent better and then catch herself and not do it. She really did change. The message had sunk in without a quarrel.

Sometimes you do need to discuss the past to explain its impact on you or to give an example of what you hope will be different in the future. But often it's just another argument. It's easy to disagree about the past: people remember different parts of it, have errors of memory, or shade or deny what really happened to let themselves off the hook. Focusing on the past—which you can't change—also takes you away from what you can influence: what happens *from now on*, three of the most hopeful words I know.

Pick a key issue and try to answer these questions for yourself: What would it look like if the other person really heard you? Respected your wishes? Acted appropriately? Spoke to you differently? Gave you what you're asking for?

Then say what you'd like from now on. Also describe any changes in thought, word, or deed that you intend to make yourself. Try to say all this in a matter-of-fact and specific way, without getting into the past or being critical. You could use a modified form of nonviolent communication: "Going forward, if we could do X, then I'd feel Y because I need Z." Or if it's appropriate to speak about the other person, the essence might be: "Going forward, if we could do X, then I think you and I would feel Y because we both need Z." If the other person gets defensive about the past, try not to get drawn into that, and return to your focus on the future.

Make Requests, Not Demands

What we communicate has three inherent elements: the content, the emotional tone, and an implicit statement about the nature of the relationship. We tend to put the most attention on crafting the content, but it's usually the emotional tone and message about the relationship that have the most impact. If you say something in the form of a command—such as "Answer the phone," "Give me that," "You must . . . ," or "You have to stop this"—that implies you get to give orders in your relationship. This rankles for most people and makes it harder to deal with the issue you're trying to resolve.

On the other hand, asking rather than demanding keeps the focus on the topic you're raising rather than triggering a side issue, and it minimizes power struggles. It acknowledges and accepts what's usually true, that you can't *make* the other person do something. This highlights the agency and responsibility of other people. If they made an agreement with you, it wasn't under duress, and they need to honor it.

Sometimes it's useful to express your request with gentleness and modesty so that it is easier for the other person to take it in. Other times it's appropriate to be serious and firm. I think of the moral weight of people like Nelson Mandela and the quality of dignity and gravity they brought to their causes. You could imagine embodying characteristics of people you admire, and sense yourself shifting into that way of being. Then, when you talk about an issue with another person, let this way of being carry you along with a self-respecting confidence. Ultimately, no matter how gentle or firm your requests are, you have the right to decide for yourself what you'll do if they're not met.

Make Clear Agreements

We often come to implicit understandings with others that work perfectly well. But if misunderstandings keep occurring or other people don't seem very committed to doing what they say they'll do, then explicit agreements can really help.

First, know what you're agreeing to. Be as specific and concrete as necessary. Pin down the meanings of fuzzy words such as "try," "help," "early," or "nice." Ask the other person what it would look like if the agreement were kept. If it's useful, write down the agreement in some way, such as an email that summarizes the new plan or a list of house rules posted on the refrigerator.

Second, explore how you could enable or support the other person to keep the agreement. Ask yourself what you could give in order to get what you want. If appropriate, ask questions such as: "What would help you to do this?" "Do you need anything from me?" "What would enable you to be consistent about this?" Sometimes the answer will be closely related to the subject of the agreement. For example, helping a co-worker with a computer issue might enable that person to get you the report you need.

At other times, what you could do might be related to the agreement in only a roundabout way. Most relationships involve some general give-and-take. Not a rigid quid pro quo, but the ordinary reality of "If you don't care about my wants, it's hard to care about yours." Whatever you think people "ought" to want to do, pragmatically it's often effective to make a kind of bargain in which you give them what they want in one area, and they give you what you want in another one.

REPAIRING RELATIONSHIPS

When riding a bike, we naturally tip one way or another and need to keep making corrections to continue down the road. It's the same with relationships, whether with a friend, co-worker, family member, or mate. At even the best of times, they require a natural process of correction—let's call it *repair*—to clear up little misunderstandings and ease points of friction. More seriously, you may need to work through conflicts, reestablish trust, or change aspects of a relationship.

If a repair is needed, that's a kind of yellow flag: something to handle, probably turning out fine. But if someone resists your efforts to mend whatever has become frayed or torn—if this person won't repair the lack of repair—that's a red flag in any significant relationship. For example, in their research on couples, John and Julie Gottman have identified repair as a primary factor in how satisfied two people will be with each other and whether they will stay together. To deal with yellow flags, and if need be any red ones, try the methods below.

Check Your Understanding

When we feel hurt by or irritated with other people, it's easy to overlook an important detail, mishear a word, misinterpret a look, or jump to the wrong conclusion. I've done this many times myself. Our reactions to others are shaped by our *appraisals*—what we see and how we interpret it—and our *attributions*: the thoughts and feelings and intentions we believe are operating inside their minds. For example, if I think my friend has ignored my invitation to lunch because he doesn't want to spend time with me, I could feel disrespected and angry. But if I learn that he never got my message about lunch and in fact would like to see me, then the mix-up is a hassle but no more than that.

It can be humbling to realize how often we have only a partial picture of what's going on, and how often we surge into a reaction that we later regret. So try to slow things down and find out what's really true. What actually happened? What was the larger context? This could put events in a more neutral or even positive light. Had the other person indeed made a specific agreement with you? Maybe there was just an honest misunderstanding. For example, perhaps a roommate thought "do the dishes" only meant fill the dishwasher, not also wipe down the stove and counter. If others try to explain things to you, does that necessarily mean they think you are stupid? They could simply be trying to be helpful, though perhaps in unnecessary ways.

Once your understanding is clear, you might decide to let something go by. Maybe it's not such a big deal, or perhaps trying to make a repair would have more costs than the benefits of whatever would be repaired. Be realistic about the capacities of other people to talk through difficult issues. Alternately, you could decide to go ahead, perhaps to take care of a small- to medium-sized issue before it becomes a big one.

Know That You Matter

Once you're clear that something needs repairing, get on your own side about it. If someone put you down, dropped the ball, acted like you didn't exist, snapped at you, promised one thing but did another, ignored you, ran over your clear boundaries, badmouthed you to others, threatened you, used you, exploited you, discriminated against you, cheated you, lied to you, or attacked you, it's normal to be bothered by it. You deserve fairness and common decency just like anyone else.

The history, the setting, and whatever you did yourself does not take away from what another person did or did not do. If your trust has been shaken—whether it's a little item or something as major as the other person's fundamental commitment to being trustworthy—that's really important to address. For example, some people are sticklers for keeping their word at work but routinely break agreements with their family, friends, or partners, even though these are actually their most important relationships. Relationships require trust, and trust comes from reliability. You have a legitimate need to find out what you can count on from others.

You're not being "weak," "needy," "hysterical," or a "whiner" if you call people on their behavior. In particular, there is nothing wrong with feeling like a "victim" if you've been victimized! Weirdly, that word has acquired a note of disdain—literally, a form of blaming the victim—when it's simply a description of what happened. If someone steps onto a crosswalk and gets hit by a drunk driver, of course that person is a victim, and there's no shame in it. Using the methods we've explored in previous chapters, try to recognize and then let go of any tendencies inside yourself to minimize or justify mistreatment of you by other people.

Speak Up

When you do talk with someone, help yourself believe that how you feel inside is important, and that others should keep their agreements and treat you with respect. Use the HEAL steps to take this sense of conviction into yourself.

Without censoring yourself, see if you can enter into a repair conversation calmly, using wise speech. This increases the chances that the other person will be receptive to what you're saying. Acknowledge your part in the issue if this is appropriate.

Let people know about their impact on you. It's understandable if you've shied away from telling others how they've hurt you, which could feel emotionally vulnerable. Nonetheless, you can hold your head high, perhaps saying something like "This did happen, it did hurt me, and I think it was wrong." Your self-respect will give weight to your efforts to repair the relationship.

You might make the other person uncomfortable, and you can judge for yourself whether that is all right or not. At times it will feel right to choose harmony instead of truth. But remember that you matter, that you are willing to be uncomfortable yourself when others try to repair with you—so you can ask the same of them—and that unresolved issues build up over time. People who repeatedly value harmony over truth often end up having neither.

Adjust the Relationship to Its True Foundation

Relationships rest on a foundation of trust, respect, and commitment. If a relationship is bigger than its foundation, it's potentially unsafe, like a pyramid turned on its head. At home or at work, if you're fair with someone who won't be fair in return, or you're open and vulnerable with someone who will use that against you later, you may need to reshape the relationship.

Suppose that you attempt to repair things and they don't improve, or that you decide for one reason or another you're not going to make that effort. Now what? Pick a relationship that you'd like to resize and imagine that it began as a circle of possibility (you could also draw this on a piece of paper). Then consider what you'd like to reduce, disengage from, or shift in a new direction. With this person, perhaps you've realized that it's best to make no more loans, to go out for coffee instead of drinks, or to avoid discussing politics. Knowing what you'd like to change—let's say it's several things—carve those aspects of the relationship out of the circle so that you end up with something that looks like a blob whose area is the size of the relationship that seems best to you. As you face what the relationship needs to be, there could be a sense of loss, dashed hopes, frustration, or disenchantment. Be mindful of this and compassionate toward yourself.

There may be things you can't alter, such as your role in the care of an aging parent or inevitable encounters with someone at work. But even if you can't change something outside of yourself, at least inside your own mind you can pull back and you can limit the impacts of others upon you.

Usually you can make some changes in a relationship. You could tell the other person what you are doing and why, or simply start acting in new ways. After this, one of three things could happen. First, your changes might prompt a serious effort at repair by the other person. If that goes well, consider expanding the relationship back to what it used to be. Second, the person or other parties such as relatives could try to pull you back into how things were in the past. Remember that you have the right to change the relationship, and remember why you did so. Third, the person could accept your new approach or simply have no say in it. For example, no one can force you to return calls or emails if you'd rather not.

Unless you have a compelling duty to a person, such as a child or a patient, you have the right to change the relationship if you want to. There's a certain toughness in this, but there may also be kindness. If deep down you don't feel comfortable or happy with how things have been going, other people usually sense that even if they don't put it into words. When you act to make a relationship better for you, sometimes it gets better for others as well.

KEY POINTS

- The times we need courage the most are often while talking with other people.

- Open, authentic communication is fundamental to any significant relationship. But it's also risky. To make it safe for yourself, recognize any real dangers, talk about talking, and separate solving problems from sharing experiences.

- Speaking wisely means saying things that are well intended, true, beneficial, timely, not harsh, and, if possible, wanted.

- To assert yourself skillfully with someone, establish the facts and know your values. Focus on the results you want, consolidate your gains, and emphasize what will happen from now on. Make requests, not demands, and establish clear agreements.

- Relationships are inherently unstable and naturally need repairs. It's a red flag if someone in a significant relationship is unwilling to repair it.

- When you make repairs, double-check what you think happened. Then get on your own side and don't be embarrassed about telling others that you've been let down, hurt, or mistreated. If necessary, shrink the relationship to a size and shape that is safe for you.

CHAPTER 11

ASPIRATION

*Tell me, what is it you plan to do with
your one wild and precious life?*

—Mary Oliver

To live is to lean into the future. We're always stretching toward one thing or another: the next person, the next task, the next sight or sound, the next breath.

This chapter focuses on meeting your need for satisfaction by reaching for and achieving results that are important to you, such as deepening an intimate relationship, getting a better job, or growing into a new way of being at home or work. In particular, we'll explore how to pursue your aims while being fundamentally at peace with whatever happens.

HONORING YOUR DREAMS

A person's path through life—day by day, year after year—is shaped by many factors. Some are not possible to control, such as your genetics or birthplace. But studies in adult development show that you still have much influence over how things turn out through how you work through cycles of stability and change, draw on teachers and mentors—and realize your dreams, including the ones you had in childhood.

What You Knew When You Were Young

Children, including very little ones, know many things even if they can't put them into words. For example, my earliest memories are colored with a watchful, wistful awareness that there was much unnecessary unhappiness in my family, with other kids, and with grown-ups in general. Nothing horrible, just a lot of needless tension, worry, and bickering. Looking back, I can see a persistent longing to understand why this was happening and to do something about it. Over time, that longing became a guiding purpose. There have been times when I pushed it to the back of my mind or forgot it entirely; in retrospect, that was when it most felt like I'd lost my way.

How about you? Think about your earliest memories and the youngest layers of your psyche. What did you see around you and what did you wish for? What did you know as a young child that you couldn't put into words back then? As you grew older, through your teens and into young adulthood, what were your ambitions, wild ideas, and secret hopes? Think about the kind of people you imagined being with, and the kind of person you imagined becoming.

Then consider what has happened to those dreams. We all have dreams we've ignored or deferred. They rest inside us, like a coin at the bottom of a well. Sometimes there are good reasons for setting a dream aside. But often, people needlessly dismiss an important dream as childish or foolish, or just keep pushing it down the road. It's so easy—poignantly, sadly easy—to talk yourself out of pursuing things that could be very fulfilling while also contributing to other people. With this in mind, let's explore the factors that can get in the way of your dreams.

THE IMPACT OF OTHERS

We're naturally influenced by the opinions of other people. Consider how your parents, friends, and teachers affected your dreams. Think about who has encouraged and helped you—and who has been dismissive, doubting, or undermining. How do the effects of all this linger on in your life today? For example, do you feel comfortable revealing your dreams to others?

Think about your attitudes toward your dreams. Then ask yourself: "Which of these attitudes are truly mine, and which have I borrowed from other people? Deep down, what do I want, what matters most to *me*?"

THE DREADED EXPERIENCE

People often swerve away from their dreams to avoid risking experiences they dread. For example, someone might not pursue a romantic relationship in order to prevent the possibility of rejection. The edges of the experiences we fear form a kind of invisible fence that limits the life we allow ourselves to have.

Take some time to think about how your life has been bounded and shaped by the experiences you've tried to avoid. Consider the things that happened to you, that you saw happening to others, or that you thought *might* happen. Also think about your temperament. For instance, some people are particularly affected by threats to connection, so it is a high priority to them to avoid experiences related to shame, such as feeling that they've done something wrong or are "a bad person." Other people are most affected by threats to safety, so they go out of their way to avoid experiences related to anxiety, such as business travel on airplanes. Think about a turning point in your life in which you veered away from pursuing a dream. At that time, what experiences were you trying to avoid? These days, do you say less than you could and play smaller than you need to in order to avoid risking certain experiences? Consider how your life would expand if you were willing to take those risks.

Dreaded experiences cast a long shadow over our dreams. But what we dread is usually rooted in childhood, and today it is much less likely, less painful, and less overwhelming than we fear. Pick something that is important to you but which you've been putting off pursuing. Next, ask yourself this: "What have I been avoiding?" It's fine to think about situations or interactions—and then try to dig deeper and find the uncomfortable, stressful *experiences* you fear you might have in those situations or interactions. Once you have identified the experiences you haven't wanted to risk, really consider these questions:

- What are the chances, actually, that events will turn out as you fear if you pursue this dream?

- Even if events did go badly, how painful an experience would you likely have? How soon would it begin to fade?

- How could you cope with the experience? What inner resources could you draw on to deal with it?

- What benefits would come to you and others from fulfilling this dream? What benefits would come from simply pursuing it? Take some moments to get a feeling for these benefits. Then ask yourself truly: are these benefits worth taking the risk of a dreaded experience?

THE ESSENCE OF YOUR DREAM

At this point, you might be thinking something like: "Well, I wanted to be a movie star as a child, and are you saying I need to be a movie star or I'll never be happy?" Not at all. The dream itself is not to be "a movie star." Being a movie star is a *means* to various ends, such as fame, the enjoyment of acting, and financial success. It is not an end in itself.

People frequently get caught up in certain means to the true ends of their dreams. But this distracts them from the end itself and often keeps it out of reach. Pick an important dream and ask yourself: what are the foundational emotional or interpersonal elements that are the essence of this dream? Could there be other ways to fulfill this essence, to achieve *the end the dream aspires to*, besides the ways you've pursued so far?

What would this be like? Whatever your fears and limitations may have been in the past, get a sense of giving yourself over to the dream today. Imagine the dream, in a sense, dreaming you—living through you and as you. Stay with the experience of this, letting it sink down into you and become stable inside you. Deep down, see if you can feel the essence of this dream. And see if you can say "yes" to it.

Love and Work and Play

To act upon your dreams in concrete ways, let's consider three key areas of life:

- **Love:** friendship, intimate relationships, raising children, compassion, kindness

- **Work:** job, career, making a home, helping others

- **Play:** creativity, imagination, fun, hobbies, delight, wonder, awe

Take a little time to assess each area, knowing they can overlap somewhat. What's going well? And what do you wish were different?

An effective way to improve each one of these areas of life is to increase the degree to which it is based upon your:

- **Likes:** activities, situations, and topics that give you pleasure

- **Talents:** your innate, natural abilities of *all* kinds, such as writing, fixing machinery, being funny, leading meetings, staying calm under pressure, cooking, or making music

- **Values:** the things that are important to you, such as children or the environment

Imagine that your likes, talents, and values are each a circle. The intersection of any two circles is good, and the intersection of all three circles is best of all. For example, if your work combines what you really like doing in its own right, what you are naturally good at, and what you most care about, then you're likely to be fulfilled and successful with it. Other factors could be relevant, such as the job market, but if you've got the fundamentals right, the rest usually follows.

For each area of your life, think about how you could realistically increase what you like, shine at, and value. In the area of love, for instance, if a long-term relationship has become less pleasurable or enjoyable, you could talk about this with your partner and explore what to do about it. Or in the area of work, there might be new ways to use your skills in service to others, such as joining the board of a nonprofit.

Honoring what *you* like, are gifted at, and feel committed to can mean taking your own path and turning away from more conventional ones. For example, there's a common notion that kids ought to know "what they want to be" when they grow up. A doctor maybe, or an artist or astronaut. But many adults don't have a specific occupation that calls to them. In fact, this could be quite natural, since our hunter-gatherer ancestors were generalists, not specialists with narrow job descriptions. When you eventually come toward the end of your life and look back over it, staying true to yourself and taking chances to honor your dreams could turn out to have been the safest bet of all.

Use the Time You Have

There's a saying that the days are long, but the years are short. An hour, especially if you're bored, can seem endless. Yet as the seconds tick by, they are gone forever. And we don't know what the future holds, including perhaps an accident or illness around the corner. As Stephen Levine has pointed out, each of us will come to a day when there is just one year to live and not know when that line has been crossed.

Life is fragile, fleeting, and precious. It's not morbid to recognize this. Rather, it's a way to celebrate the days we do have, and commit to making the best of them.

Many years ago, I was moaning and groaning to my friend Tom about how long it was going to take to finish grad school and fulfill all the postdoctoral requirements to become a psychologist. I was in my mid-thirties and tired of still being a student. I complained that I might even be forty years old, which seemed ancient at the time, before I was licensed. Tom asked, "Do you plan on being forty?" Startled, I said, "Um, yes, I hope so." "Well, then," he went on, "how do you want it to be?"

I've thought about Tom's questions many times since. Sometimes something is just not possible. For example, it may be too late to change a career or have a child. But more often than not, people presume too easily and too quickly that an opportunity has irrevocably passed.

Consider a long-standing desire—such as starting a business, riding horses again, getting back into a romantic relationship, or seeing the Parthenon—and then pick an age five or ten years from now. Ask yourself: "Do I plan on being that age? How do I want it to be?"

Imagine you're approaching the end of your life and looking back at it. What will you be glad you've done with the days that remain to you?

As you consider this, you might find that there's a fire in your belly for one more big push in your career or one more big project. Or perhaps something smaller is calling to you: volunteering at the hospital, meditating more regularly, making peace with a relative, going back to church, seeing the Grand Canyon, learning to play the piano, moving closer to grandchildren, or getting involved in local politics. Or maybe what really matters to you is not a specific thing but rather a way of being, such as becoming more carefree, self-accepting, loving, and playful.

Whatever it is that calls you, make it important to you. You could write it down, make a collage about it, or bring it to mind each day. Then plan the steps that will make it happen for real, and imagine the good things that will come to you and others if you do these steps. Use the HEAL process to repeatedly take in this association between actions and rewards so that you will take these steps. Feel a sense of commitment and help that sink in, too. And then act to make your dream a reality. Try to value each day as literally a once-in-a-lifetime opportunity.

ASPIRING WITHOUT ATTACHMENT

Many years ago, I spent a week rock climbing in Colorado with my friend Bob and our guide, Dave. On the first day, I thrashed and failed on an intermediate climb (graded 5.8), which Bob scooted right up. Afterward, Dave asked us what our goals were for the week. I said, "I want to climb 5.11," which is seriously hard. Bob, a very determined, ambitious, competitive guy—the same Bob in the chapter on grit who nearly froze to death breaking a trail for us through soft snow—burst out: "You're crazy, you'll never do it, and then you'll feel bad about yourself!" Bob was on my side and wanted to protect me from the disappointment and embarrassment he would feel in my place. But for me it was the *opposite*. Because this was such an outlandish goal, it was "win-win" to pursue it: if things didn't work out, there'd be no shame, and if I succeeded, it would feel great.

We climbed every day with Dave, and I started getting better. By midweek, my goal didn't seem *quite* so crazy, and Bob got excited that this might actually happen. On the very last day, I started up a solid 5.11 crack, made it to the top without a fall, and was completely thrilled.

This has been such an example for me of what it's like to *aspire without attachment*—to dream big dreams and pursue them with commitment while also being at peace with whatever happens. But easier said than done. How do we go full throttle . . . while staying in the green zone?

Have a Growth Mindset

The term "growth mindset" comes from Carol Dweck's research on people who focus more on their efforts to learn and grow than on the specific results they've achieved. For example, if a person is in a tennis game against a much better player, the goal could shift from winning points to improving the backhand. People with a growth mindset tend to be happier, more resilient, and more successful. Think of a big goal and what it would feel like to redefine success in terms of developing new skills, understanding others better, or acquiring knowledge. Then, no matter what occurs, you've still succeeded.

This attitude makes it easier to aim high. It's quite often possible to accomplish something that's a lot more meaningful with just a little more effort. Big goals focus the mind, inspire us, and motivate sustained work. It's counterintuitive, but the bigger the goal, the more likely it could be that you will reach it.

Know That It's All Right to Fail

Failure happens. Not everything works out. There's a story about a Zen master who had helped many people and accomplished many things. Toward the end of his life, he was asked how he felt about all that he'd done. He smiled ruefully and said, "One failure after another." No one succeeds in a big way without sometimes failing in a big way. If you fail, you'll be in good company.

How would it feel if you aimed high but fell short? There could be disappointment, a sense of wasted effort, and fears about looking bad in the eyes of others. And—would you still be basically all right? Would your life go on, would your friends still like you, and would you have other opportunities? Because of its negativity bias, the brain fixates on the handful of tiles in reality's mosaic that will indeed flash red if you fail. Meanwhile, it downplays the many more tiles that will stay a steady green, such as the love of others, the comfort in your bed, and the dignity and self-respect in knowing you tried hard and kept faith with yourself. In your heart, see if you can accept whatever happens. You may not like it, but you can be all right with it.

People sometimes worry that if they accept failure, they'll become complacent and give up. Actually, the more willing you are to fail, the more likely you are to succeed. The fear of failure is burdensome, like a brick in your backpack as you climb up the road of life, and preoccupations with failure bind attention and energy. If you accept the possibility of defeat, you improve the chance of victory.

Don't Take It Too Personally

Try to appreciate that many of the causes of success or failure don't have your name on them. For example, my own efforts helped me climb 5.11 in Colorado, but many other factors—Dave's skills as a guide, Bob's supportive friendship, and good weather on our last day—had nothing to do with me. The perhaps uncomfortable reality is that much of what shapes our lives is beyond our control, including environmental, genetic, historical, cultural, and economic factors. Major events are often dictated by random chance—a lucky meeting, where a résumé landed in a pile, a careless driver drifting into another lane.

If a person gets caught up in comparisons to others, pulling for approval, or quarreling over crumbs of credit, then "me, myself, and I" have taken over. So try to hold the sense of self lightly. The preoccupation with "self" feels tense and undermines support from others. Plus it makes us attach stressfully and possessively to particular results—like Gollum in *The Lord of the Rings* clinging to "my *Precious!*"

Let Aspiration Carry You Along

One way to fulfill an aspiration is to push toward it as if it were outside you, in the distance, like scratching and clawing up a mountain. That might work for a while, but it's exhausting. The other way is to give yourself over to the aspiration and let it *pull* you along, like rafting downstream in a river. In effect, you are using your will to surrender to your aspiration, which is both more comfortable and more sustainable.

To get a sense of this, pick an aspiration. Imagine it outside of you, separate from you, off in the distance as a goal that you are pushing and straining toward. Notice how this feels. Then imagine the aspiration as a purpose that is already joined with you, and is lifting and energizing and carrying you along. Now, notice how *this* feels. For this particular aspiration, use the HEAL steps to internalize this second way of relating to it. Pick other aspirations and get a sense of being lifted and carried by them. Enrich and absorb these experiences so that the second approach to aspiration becomes habitual for you.

MAKING YOUR OFFERING

Many of the ways that we love, work, and play are a kind of offering to others. Think about what you give, large and small, at home, on the job, to friends, to strangers, and to the wider world. We all offer so much each day, even if we don't realize it in the moment.

When you look at the things you do as offerings, they feel simpler, lighter, and more heartfelt. Even routine, seemingly trivial tasks take on new meaning and value. There's less sense of pressure. Instead of worrying about how others might respond, the focus shifts to doing what you can yourself—as I learned many years ago when speaking with a friend, an aspiring Zen priest. He was about to give his first talk at the center in San Francisco where he was training, which was very important, even sacred, to him. I had read in the news that homeless people would come in off the street to the meditation hall simply because they wanted to be in a warm and safe place, not because they were interested in Buddhism. In a teasing, provocative way, I asked him how he felt about people in the audience not actually caring about what he was saying. He looked at me like I'd missed the point.

We were sitting facing each other, and he made a gesture as if he were placing something at my feet. "I just make the offering," he said. "I try to create a good talk. Maybe tell a joke to keep it interesting. But after that it's out of my hands. What they do with it is up to them." He didn't say this coldly or dismissively, like he didn't care about other people. He was just being calm and realistic. And by not trying to force others to appreciate what he was saying, he would actually have a better chance of reaching them.

I think about the lesson of the fruit tree in my backyard. We can pick a sturdy sapling, plant it well, and water it over the years—but we can't force it to produce an apple. We can tend to the causes but can't control the results. All we can do is make the offering.

Know *What* You're Offering

It's easy to lose sight of exactly what you want to offer, especially in complex situations or relationships. You might feel pressured by what others want you to do, or you could take for granted a role you acquired in early adulthood. Consequently, it can help to clarify for yourself what is and is *not* your task, job, duty, or purpose with a particular person or setting. For example, when Jan and I became parents, we had to figure out who was going to do what. I'm the sort of person who makes to-do lists, and it helped me to develop a mental job description for myself as a father and husband. Then I knew what to do each day and didn't obsess over whether I'd dropped the ball.

This may sound a little mechanical, but in practice it feels natural, informal, and flexible—and oh so clarifying and freeing. There is a peacefulness in knowing that you have done your part and everything else is not your responsibility.

Let's say you have a relationship with a co-worker, friend, or family member. What's for you to do—and what's for them to do? For example, with teenage children, you could decide that it is your job to insist that they do their homework, to help them as needed, and to impose consequences if they skip classes. But only they can actually learn anything from school. Or consider a romantic partner. You can give love, attention, and affection—but, poignant as it is, love for you is the other person's offering to give.

People often get caught up in trying to make something happen inside the black box of another person's mind: getting someone to think, feel, or care in a certain way. So much frustration and conflict comes from this. As appropriate, you can give your opinions and recommendations, and the reasons for them. That's your offering. The rest is the other person's decision.

In particular, we cannot *make* others happy—even our own children. Nonetheless, it's common to experience a burdensome sense of responsibility for the mood or behavior of particular people, especially family members. We can take reasonable steps, ranging from asking how someone is feeling to taking a child to a therapist. But as heart-wrenching as it may be, what others do with what we offer is up to them.

Or let's say that you have a project at work. Think about all that you can and should do . . . and then draw a line around it. That's your offering. The same with your career in general. Show up, prepare, learn, put in the hours, be consistent, do your job. Then you can know that whatever your trajectory of success may be in this life, a lack of effort did not lower it. The rest is up to so many other factors. You can give a great sales pitch, but you can't make a prospect say yes. You can open a shop, but you can't make people come into it. Try not to let a preoccupation with what's out of your hands get in the way of taking care of what's in your reach each day.

Find Fertile Ground

Sometimes we make an offering but it's like casting seeds on stony soil. Consider your activities and relationships, and see if there are any of these indicators of less than fertile ground:

- Giving much more than you're getting in a friendship

- Needing to make extreme efforts to keep a business afloat

- Helping people who don't want to be helped

- Trying to make something better keeps making it worse

- Picking the same sort of person and expecting different results

- Fighting hard to gain crumbs

- Communicating into what feels like a vacuum

- Tackling symptoms without changing disease or dysfunction

When you pour yourself into something that's not bearing much fruit, it can feel sad and disappointing. You may want to keep pushing and hope you'll finally turn a corner. This might work out. But the best predictor of the future is usually the past. See if you know in your heart that things are not likely to get better. There is such a thing as healthy disenchantment, which can feel like waking up from a kind of spell. Each of us has many gifts but limited time. Effort spent trying to grow roses in cement is effort that would produce better results elsewhere for both you and others.

Think about different relationships, settings, or activities that might provide more fertile ground. No guarantees, but better odds. Often there is an intuition that says, "Try this." Consider your temperament, natural gifts, and deep nature: Who could use what you've got? What settings and activities pull the best out of you? What kind of person always seems to appreciate you? Where do you feel most at home?

Think about a time in your life when you really blossomed. Perhaps it was a week each summer at your aunt's farm, a play in high school, a talk given at a work conference, or a passionate letter to the editor. Perhaps it was when you took a group of children camping, did a financial analysis, worked in a stable, brought food to a homeless shelter, or built a website. When you identify such a time, look closely at its characteristics. What were the best things about it?

Then consider how you might be able to develop some of these characteristics in your current relationships, settings, and activities—helping them to become more fertile ground for you. Also consider how you could step into a new relationship, setting, or activity that would be a good fit for you: nurturing and appreciative, with room to breathe and room to grow. If it is fine to wish such fertile ground for your child or for your friend, it is also fine to seek it for yourself—in your one wild and precious life.

KEY POINTS

- When we are young, we have hopes and dreams for the life we'd like to have. What has happened to your own dreams along the way?

- People swerve away from their dreams for a variety of reasons. In particular, they try to avoid "dreaded experiences." Consider how it could enlarge your life to risk these experiences.

- In love, work, and play, find the sweet spot at the intersection of three circles: what you enjoy, what you're talented at, and what you care about.

- The days may be long, but the years are short. Use the time that you have.

- To aim high while being at peace with the results, have a growth mindset, know that it's all right to fail, and don't take what happens too personally.

- Offer what you can, and know that after that it's out of your hands.

CHAPTER 12

GENEROSITY

*Who gives, one's virtues shall
increase.*

—Digha Nikaya, 2.197

Like most young children, Forrest liked sweets. One time when he was in preschool, we went out to dinner at a local restaurant, and an older man and woman at the next table watched us with amusement. When the check arrived with a red-striped peppermint, I gave it to Forrest and he started eagerly unwrapping it. As a joke, the man sitting next to us reached out his hand and asked, "Can I have your candy?" We all expected Forrest to hold on to it possessively. Instead, he looked at the man for a few seconds—and handed him the peppermint. The man was startled, and then he gave Forrest a huge smile as he said, "Oh no, thank you, but you keep it." Other diners nearby had been watching and there was an audible "Awwwwwww" around us. It was just a little moment, just a little boy in a crowded restaurant, but we could all relate to the generosity in it.

At first glance, generosity may not seem like a mental resource, but it strengthens you with a sense of the fullness that's already inside you while also connecting you with other people. Generosity to them is a gift to you along the way, giving you even more to offer in a positive cycle.

We've already explored many ways to fill up your own cup, which gives you more that you can place in the cups—and hands and hearts—of others. In this chapter, we'll begin with recognizing and expanding generosity in daily life. Next, we'll see how to bring equanimity to compassion so that you can keep giving without becoming depleted. Then we'll dive into one of the most important but hardest ways to give, which is to forgive others and yourself. We'll conclude with the widest expression of generosity: expanding the circle of "us" to include more and more of "them."

EVERYDAY GIVING

The essence of generosity is *altruism*, giving without expecting anything in return. As I said in the chapter on confidence, altruism is rare in nature, since freeloaders can exploit generosity. The great exception to this rule is our own species, *Homo sapiens*. The evolving social capabilities of our ancestors gave them increasingly powerful ways to recognize and punish freeloaders. Meanwhile, the generosity of one individual—sharing food, defending against aggression by outsiders—could increase the chances of survival of others with whom that person shared genes. Tendencies toward altruism were both protected and valuable, and they became woven into our DNA. In many ways, we are *Homo beneficus*: the generous human.

As a result, generosity is everywhere around us. Obvious examples include leaving a tip in the jar at a coffee shop or sending a check to a charity, but also consider all the nonfinancial kinds of giving. Think about a typical day and the many times you offer your attention, patience, help, or encouragement. Perhaps you commiserate with a co-worker who's had a hard day, pick up a piece of trash on the sidewalk, or help organize a school event. With children, relatives, friends, or your partner, you probably do things that are not your preference in the moment and stretch to take others into account.

Of course, this does not mean giving because you've been pressured, used, or manipulated. If your generosity is forced, that's harmful to you. Further, it's a lost opportunity for others who could make better use of what you've been offering. When you know that you'll protect yourself from overgiving, it feels safe to be even more generous. So give yourself permission to make changes if a relationship is out of balance, and give what *you* want to give.

Whatever it is that you *do* give is not lessened by what you don't give, nor is it lessened by what you receive from others. As you go through your day, notice some of the many things you give. Slow down to feel what it's like to be generous, and let the sense of this sink into you. Try to recognize yourself as a giving, generous person, and notice what it feels like inside to see yourself in this way. There could be an opening in your heart, a sense of worth, and love. You can enjoy a happiness in giving that helps to sustain it.

When we're unable to give what we have to offer, it aches inside. There is love but no one to give it to; there is talent but no place to use it. A quiet sadness in many people comes from feeling that the contributions they could make have no outlet. It's important to find channels through which your gifts can flow, especially the seemingly small ones in daily life. It's striking how simple it can be to add to the lives of other people, even just by offering a little praise or giving your full attention for longer than usual. You could pick someone and look for ways to be particularly appreciative or helpful; see how this feels for you, and see what happens for the other person.

Think about a friend, family member, or co-worker. Is there anything you'd like to give—such as loving warmth, practical help, or an apology—yet you're holding back? Maybe there's a good reason. But sometimes we're so self-absorbed about what we want to give—

ruminating about how people will react, fixing every little detail, or waiting for the absolutely perfect right time—that we get in our own way. See what happens when you pull attention out of yourself and place it on and *in* other people. What do they need, what do they long for, where are they hurting, and how could you help?

COMPASSION WITH EQUANIMITY

The word "compassion" comes from the Latin roots *com* and *pati*, which mean "to suffer *with*." We add the suffering of others to our own, a gift at the heart of being human. How can we be moved by the sorrows of others without becoming flooded, drained, or burned out?

To sustain compassion, we need *equanimity*, a kind of inner shock absorber between the core of your being and whatever is passing through awareness. Some experiences are first darts, such as feeling the suffering of others. With equanimity, these don't become second darts that push you into the Reactive red zone. You can see the bigger picture, including the sweet amidst the bitter, and the many causes—most of them impersonal—that lead to suffering. For example, a teacher of mine once described taking a small boat down the Ganges at dawn and seeing beautiful rose-lit towers on the left and smoking funeral pyres on the right. She talked about the need to develop a heart that's wide enough to include both of these aspects of life and wise enough to hold them in balance. With equanimity, you can feel the pain of others without being swept away by it—which helps you open to it even more fully.

In these pages, we've explored many ways to develop equanimity in general. To bring equanimity alongside compassion, it helps to stay grounded in your body, aware of the sensations of breathing as you feel the pain of other people. Reflect on the fact that the suffering is part of a vast web of causes and effects. Not to justify or diminish it, but to see the bigger picture with acceptance and insight. Notice what it is like to be deeply touched by another person while at the same time having an inner stability of calm awareness. Let this way of being establish itself in you so you can draw upon it in the future.

As you face the enormity of the suffering in this world, you might feel flooded with a sense of despair at the impossibility of ever doing enough. If this happens, it can help to take some kind of action, since action eases despair. There's a story about two people walking down miles of ocean beach on which thousands of starfish had been washed up by the tide and were now dying in the sun. One of them reached down every few steps to toss a starfish back into the water. After a while, the other one said, "There are so many, what you're doing doesn't make any difference." The first person replied, "It makes a world of difference to the ones I pick up."

Think about the people in your life, including those you don't know well. Could you make a difference to someone? Seemingly little things can be very touching. Consider humanity in general as well as nonhuman animals, and see if something is calling to you. Not to burden you, but to push back against helplessness and despair, and to know that you have returned another starfish to the sea.

Also take some time to reflect on what you have already done to help others and on what you are currently doing. Imagine how all this has rippled out into the world in ways seen and unseen. The truth of what you have given rests alongside the truth that there is still so much suffering, and knowing the one will help your heart stay open to the other.

FORGIVING OTHERS—AND YOURSELF

Let's say someone truly mistreated you or made a serious mistake—or did this to others. After you deal with the consequences and assert yourself as you judge best, then what? If it seems right, you could draw upon the generosity of forgiveness.

Full Pardon Forgiveness

I think there are two kinds of forgiveness. In the first of these, you give someone a *full pardon*. It's a complete pass for whatever happened, and you wipe the slate clean. You don't seek compensation, punishment, or repayment of debts. You could continue to believe that what happened was unjust, morally wrong, or a crime, while also having good wishes, even love, toward the other person. The wheels of justice may still need to turn in their impersonal way, but in your heart you carry no grudge or grievance. You have some understanding of the forces that led people to do what they did. You feel compassion for them, perhaps with the sense that their actions were driven by their suffering. You value their good qualities as human beings, and are willing to give relationships a fresh start.

While any kind of forgiveness is given unilaterally, as a personal choice, it's affected by what others do. It's easier to give a full pardon to people who have admitted what they did, shown remorse, made amends, and taken steps to prevent anything similar in the future.

Nonetheless, even if others have taken these steps—and especially if they haven't—a full pardon may just not feel right to you. You may believe that no amount of contrition can ever wipe the slate fully clean. Or you could feel that a full pardon *might* be possible someday, but you're not yet ready for it. Perhaps you're still in shock, the wound is too fresh, the grieving is too intense. Maybe you want to take some time to be sure that you're not being manipulated by someone who wrongs you, begs forgiveness . . . and then does it again. Or to be sure that you're not moving to a full pardon due to others who tell you that what happened wasn't so bad and push you to get over it.

Sometimes, for whatever reason, a full pardon is out of the question. But you still don't want to be preoccupied by what happened, ruminating about it with hurt and anger.

Disentangled Forgiveness

This is where *disentangled forgiveness* is very useful. There is no presumption of a moral pass, compassion, or return to full relationship. It's a much lower bar. The person you are forgiving in this way may in fact keep denying that anything bad happened or even blame you for it. Nonetheless, you are disentangling yourself, finding some closure and release related to the issue, and moving on emotionally. You're trying to help yourself deal with things from the Responsive mode—the green zone—no matter what the other person does.

With this kind of forgiveness, you may still pursue compensation or punishment as a matter of justice, yet you would do so with no sense of malice or vengeance. You might have to deal with the consequences of what the other person did as a kind of first dart, but you don't add second darts of recrimination, resentment, or revving up your family and friends. If you limit, shrink, or end your relationships with certain people, you do it to protect yourself, not to hurt those who have hurt you. When you remember what happened, it may still sting, but your attention doesn't keep returning to it like a tongue to a cold sore. You are no longer carrying it around.

People often start with disentangled forgiveness and eventually move to a full pardon. But there's no assumption that this will occur. Still, if forgiveness is like a house with two floors, knowing that you're not obligated to climb up to the second one—a full pardon—makes it easier to enter the house at all.

Foundations for Forgiveness

Both kinds of forgiveness are supported by three underlying conditions. First, the time needs to be ripe. Forgiveness is a process akin to Elisabeth Kübler-Ross's stages of grief:

- **Denial:** "I can't believe that happened."

- **Anger:** "How dare you treat me that way!"

- **Bargaining:** "Look, just admit you made a mistake and we'll be fine."

- **Depression:** "I feel sad and hurt and frustrated."

- **Acceptance:** "What happened was bad, but it is what it is, and I want to move on."

The last stage is the transition into active forgiveness. As you enter it, use the HEAL steps to help this acceptance become established in you.

Second, truth needs to be told. You can't forgive something fully if you haven't named it fully: the facts of what happened, how it impacted you and others, and how it felt way down deep inside. Know your relevant values, and ask yourself, "What do I think was wrong here, and why?" In your mind, establish what you believe without minimizing it or exaggerating it. Have compassion for how all this landed on you. In other words, tell the truth to yourself.

Additionally, if you want, tell some or all of it to others. When you've been wronged, the sense of having others stand with you—of having allies who are bearing witness even if there's nothing else they can do—is calming, nurturing, and healing. As you feel their understanding and caring, open to it and receive it into yourself, taking it in like a soothing balm.

Then, if it seems safe enough, you could try to talk with the person you want to forgive, and the methods in Chapters 9 and 10 will be helpful. After you say what happened and how it affected you, the other person might take a breath and genuinely apologize. But if you are met with a lot of resistance, such as excuses or counter-accusations about you, ask yourself: "What do I want to say *for my own sake* here?" This is not about persuading or changing the other person, which is out of your control. It's about going on record, feeling free and unafraid, and standing up for yourself—all of which can help you move on to forgiveness.

Third, recognize the costs of *not* forgiving the other person. It pains me to admit the price I've paid for resentment and bitterness in my own life and to admit how these attitudes have also harmed other people. Feeling put upon and aggrieved can become a too-familiar theme in a person's relationships.

Disentangling Yourself

On these foundations, when you feel ready, you can move into disentangled forgiveness. Here are some good ways to do this.

CHOOSE TO FORGIVE

Clearly decide that you are going to forgive. Try to stay focused on the benefits to you and others of doing this. Be mindful of the hidden rewards—what therapists call *secondary gains*—that can keep a person tangled up with grievances, such as the pleasures of righteous anger.

CONSIDER THEIR PERSPECTIVE

Without minimizing what the other people did, try to see events through their eyes. What led to their actions? Perhaps their values and standards are different from yours. Maybe what to you was a major violation was to them not a misdeed at all. You can continue to believe in your personal values while also recognizing that others can be acting in good faith in their own minds.

Additionally, they may have been hungry, tired, ill, upset, or stressed. Maybe they recently received terrible news. Maybe they just didn't know better. Considering these possibilities doesn't excuse bad behavior, but seeks to understand it more fully in order to feel more peaceful about it.

TAKE RESPONSIBILITY FOR YOUR EXPERIENCE

Others are responsible for what they do, but we are the source of our reactions to it. If the same mistreatment or injustice landed on ten people from around the world, there would be differences in how they experienced it. This doesn't mean that someone's reactions are inappropriate, but that they're shaped by that person's own mind. Recognizing this doesn't invalidate your experience but holds it more lightly, which helps untangle you from it.

KNOW WHAT YOU'RE GOING TO DO

Depending on what happened, you could decide to write a letter, skip a family gathering, call a lawyer, stop confiding in someone, use a different plumber, or simply watch and wait. Other people will do whatever they do; meanwhile, focus on your own actions. Knowing what your plan is, and that you *have* a plan and are not helpless, is calming and centering, and this makes more room in your mind for forgiveness.

LET GO OF ANY ILL WILL

With disentangled forgiveness, you may not like the people who wronged you, and you may be taking action against them. But you are letting go of any hostility or vindictiveness.

To do this, be aware of what resentment feels like in your body, and then use long exhalations to relax and to release these sensations. Visualize ill will as a heavy stone that you are setting down. You might like to pick up a real stone, imagine that it contains all of your desires for vengeance, and then drop it or throw it far, far away. You could write a letter that you'll never send—perhaps full of bitterness, scorn, and punishing rage—and then cut it into small pieces, burn it, and cast the ashes to the wind. Use the Link step in HEAL to bring "antidote" experiences into ill will to ease and gradually replace it. For instance, be aware of resentment off to the side of your mind while a sense of others who care about you is large and powerful.

As you rest increasingly in disentangled forgiveness, know what it feels like. Enrich this experience by staying with it, letting it fill your mind, sensing it in your body, exploring what feels new or fresh about it, and recognizing how it is relevant and important to you. Absorb it by sensing that forgiveness is sinking into you and by focusing on what feels good about it. Take a breath, and step out of the tangles.

Giving a Full Pardon

Years ago, when our kids were little, a neighbor's tall tree fell into our backyard and knocked down the fence between us. We asked him to take care of the tree and he agreed, but weeks and then months passed with no action. I'd talk with him and he'd smile and promise to deal with it, but nothing happened. It was getting ridiculous and I was getting mad. But that wasn't helping my family or me, and I started moving into disentangled forgiveness. I thought, "It was just a big tree, not our house burning down," and I didn't need to add my own anger to the simple facts of the situation. This forgiveness was aided by knowing what I was going to do—which included writing the neighbor a polite but firm letter saying that our insurance company would be contacting him. The day after he received the letter, about five months after the tree fell, there was a crew in our backyard to remove it.

But it was still very awkward between us, and I wanted to find my way to a full pardon. So I thought about him as a person, not as a two-dimensional "jerk of a neighbor." He was an older man living alone in a broken-down house surrounded by dry grass and weeds, and no one ever visited him. I remembered that he was fond of the raccoons that came into his yard, and he set out food for them. On Halloween when our kids came to his door, he showered them with candy. I could see that he had a good heart, and was probably worried about money and the cost of removing the tree, plus dealing with loneliness and aging. I felt compassion for him, with some understanding of the many factors that kept the tree in our backyard. I recalled his halting attempt at an apology, and winced at the memory of brushing it aside. I imagined what a tiny speck that tree would be when seen from outer space. I felt the moral weight of this teaching from the Buddha:

There are those who do not realize that one day we all must die,
but those who do realize this, settle their quarrels.

Through these steps, I came to a full pardon, and we lived beside each other with a neighborly friendliness. When he did die a few years later, I felt sad about it, and glad that I'd come to peace with him. When I look back at my neighbor and the tree, there are some good lessons in it.

SEE THE WHOLE PERSON

When we're appalled, hurt, or angry, it's easy to reduce people to the one terrible thing they did. But around that is so much else: other intentions that were good, a whole complex life history, and their own hopes and dreams. When we see the whole, it's not as hard to forgive the part. Everyone suffers, including the people who wrong us. Whatever they did is not negated or excused by their pain and loss and stress, but compassion for the load they carry makes it easier to forgive the load they put on you. As Henry Wadsworth Longfellow wrote: "If we could read the secret history of our enemies, we should find in each [person's] life sorrow and suffering enough to disarm any hostility."

Sometimes people will give you a direct and sincere apology. In other cases, they won't admit any fault but you can see a change of heart in their actions. Try to see their efforts—even if implicit or imperfect—to reach out, mend what's been torn, and ask you for forgiveness.

TAKE A WIDE VIEW

Place whatever happened in the context of your whole life, including your many relationships and activities. Think about the many minutes and years—and the many parts—of your life that will be untouched and unharmed by what occurred. Take an even wider view, and try to see what happened as a swirling collection of events swept along by many factors, like an eddy in a vast river of causes. This perspective may seem abstract at first, but it will become a felt recognition of the truth of what you are forgiving: many parts, many causes, continually changing. Seeing and feeling this draws you naturally into letting go, which aids full pardon forgiveness.

Forgiving Yourself

Many people find it much easier to forgive others than to forgive themselves. Compassion, sense of perspective, seeing the whole person, letting go, wiping the slate clean: can you give these things as generously to yourself as you give them to others?

The first step toward forgiving yourself is *taking responsibility for what you did*. Admit everything—certainly to yourself, and perhaps to someone else. It's hard to give a full pardon to people if they're still arguing about whether they did anything wrong. Similarly, it's impossible to give one to yourself without taking maximum reasonable responsibility for what happened. Accepting what you *are* responsible for helps you to know—and if need be, to assert to others—what you are *not* responsible for. For example, if what you did was a 3 on the 0–10 scale of wrongdoing, own that it was indeed a 3 while knowing that it wasn't a 10.

As you take responsibility, let yourself *feel appropriate remorse*. You get to decide what's appropriate, in proportion to what you are responsible for. If you are responsible for a 3 on the wrongdoing scale, it's appropriate to feel a 3 on the 0–10 remorse scale—but not a 4, let alone a 10. Opening to remorse allows it to flow through you. There is often a spiral of remorse in which we feel and release the surface layer . . . then a deeper layer . . . and then the deepest layer of all. Experiencing remorse fully creates a kind of space in which you can forgive yourself.

Meanwhile, *repair and make amends as best you can.* Clean up the mess if possible, go the extra mile, and act with integrity from this point forward. Others may reject your efforts or doubt your sincerity. As time passes and you keep demonstrating your good intentions, they could move toward disentangled forgiveness or even a full pardon. But the point isn't to prove yourself or gain their approval. You're doing what's right for its own sake.

Also *see the larger causes of your actions.* In your mind, on paper, or through speaking with someone, reflect on how your behavior was in some ways the result of your life history, culture, health, temperament, the models that your parents and others provided, pressures and stresses on you, and what was happening just before whatever you did. Consider the evolution of your brain and how the (metaphorical) lizard, mouse, and monkey inside you shaped your actions. See what you did as an eddy in a river of causes that stretches *way* upstream . . . generations upstream through your parents and their parents and theirs, reaching back centuries and millennia and even upstream of that. It's humbling but also freeing to look at things this way. Whatever you did was the result of many forces, so by definition it wasn't *all* your fault. And no matter how big it was, in the sweep of time and space it's such a tiny part of everything.

If you can, *ask for forgiveness.* This may feel vulnerable and uncomfortable, but speaking from the heart usually opens the hearts of others. If it's not possible to ask the individual directly, ask others who were involved for the forgiveness or understanding they can offer. You might imagine friends, relatives, or other beings—alive today or no longer with you—sitting with you and saying that they forgive you. If it's meaningful to you, you could ask God to forgive you.

Finally, *forgive yourself.* You could say the words inside your mind, "I forgive you." Or write yourself a letter of forgiveness. On different occasions I've essentially said to myself: "Rick, you blew it. You really hurt someone. But you've taken responsibility, been fully remorseful, and done everything you can to fix things. You need to make sure you never do it again. And—you are forgiven. I forgive you. I forgive myself." Find your own words, and as you say them to yourself, feel a release and an easing sinking into you. Give yourself a fresh start. Give yourself the gift of a full pardon.

WIDENING THE CIRCLE OF US

As we go through the day, we're routinely sorting people into two clusters: like me and not like me, those who belong to the same groups I belong to (perhaps based on gender, ethnicity, religion, or political beliefs) and those who do not, "us" and "them." Studies show that we tend to be generous to "us" and critical, dismissive, and hostile toward "them." Us-against-them conflicts play out in families, schoolyards, office politics, public policy, and cold and hot wars. We're tribal beings, shaped by millions of years of evolution to be cooperative with us while being suspicious and aggressive toward them.

Think about the "thems" in your life, such as the relatives you don't care for, people who have a different race or religion, or those on the other side of the political divide. As you bring them to mind, notice any sense of threat, tension, or guarding. For individuals, the "them-ing" of others is stressful, blocks opportunities for friendship and teamwork, and fuels conflicts. For humanity as a whole, "us" against "them" worked in the Stone Age, but with billions of people now living interdependently together, hurting them is hurting us. Expanding your circle of "us" is not just generous to others, it's good for you as well.

To expand the circle of us, start by thinking about someone who cares about you, and then take some time to let yourself feel appreciated, liked, or cherished. Next, bring to mind someone who is suffering, and have compassion. Open your heart and feel love flowing in and out.

Then think about a group you belong to. Explore the sense of *us* itself: what it feels like in your body, and related thoughts, emotions, attitudes, and intentions. Be aware of any feelings of camaraderie, friendliness, or loyalty toward us.

Knowing what us feels like, start expanding your circle of us to include more and more people. Consider similarities between you and others you've thought were different, perhaps with thoughts such as: "You, too, get a headache sometimes . . . You also enjoy eating good food . . . Like me, you love your children . . . Like everyone does, you and I both will die someday." Pick a similarity and imagine all the people in the world who share it standing together with you as an us. Try this with other similarities as well.

Pick a group of people you feel threatened by or angry at. Then think about them as young children. Consider the forces that shaped them into the adults they are today. Reflect on how their lives, like yours, have been hard in various ways. Get a sense of their burdens, worries, losses, and pain. Find compassion for them. Recognize how we are all brought together as one great "us" by the suffering we share.

Imagine a circle of us that contains the people who are closest to you. Then expand the sense of us to include more and more people . . . in your extended family . . . neighborhood . . . networks of friends . . . workplace . . . city . . . state . . . country . . . continent . . . world. People who are like you and people who are not. People you fear or oppose. The rich and the poor, the old and the young, the known and unknown. Widening the circle to include everyone. Expanding it further to include all life . . . the creatures of the land, the sea, and the air . . . plants and microbes . . . all of us living together on one blue-green planet. All of *us*.

• • •

Speaking of circles, we have come all the way back to where we began: compassion for yourself and others. True compassion is active, not passive; it leans toward what hurts and wants to help. To offer this help generously, you give from what's inside you, from inner strengths such as grit, gratitude, and others we've explored together. As you grow more, you give more. As you give, the world gives back—helping you become even more resilient.

KEY POINTS

- Humans are naturally altruistic. Most generosity does not involve money. Appreciating yourself as a giver helps you keep giving.

- To give compassion without being overwhelmed by the suffering of others, we need equanimity, which can be cultivated by seeing suffering in its larger context, taking action as best you can, and recognizing what you have already done.

- There are two ways to give forgiveness. Without offering someone a full pardon, you can still disentangle yourself from resentment by considering that person's perspective, deliberately choosing to forgive, and letting go of ill will.

- To give a full pardon, think about the person who wronged you as a whole human being with many parts and deep down a good heart. Also have compassion, recognize remorse, and see whatever happened as an eddy in a vast river of causes.

- To give yourself a full pardon, take responsibility for whatever you did, feel appropriate remorse, make amends, ask for forgiveness, and actively forgive yourself.

- Many times a day, we sort people into two groups. We tend to cooperate with "us" but fear and attack "them." It is generous to expand the circle of us to include them, and it is necessary for all of us to live together in peace.

- As you grow inner strengths such as compassion and courage, you develop resilient well-being. This gives you more that you can give to others, and then they have more to give you, in a beautiful upward spiral.

Well-being, resilience, and the specific topics of the twelve chapters in this book are large subjects, and many individuals and organizations have contributed in these areas. Here is a partial listing of papers, books, websites, and organizations that may interest you.

GENERAL BACKGROUND

American Psychological Association, "The Road to Resilience" (www.apa .org/helpcenter/road-resilience.aspx)

Block, Jeanne H., and Jack Block. "The role of ego-control and ego-resiliency in the organization of behavior." In *Development of cognition, affect, and social relations: The Minnesota symposia on child psychology,* vol. 13, pp. 39–101. 1980.

Burton, Nicola W., Ken I. Pakenham, and Wendy J. Brown. "Feasibility and effectiveness of psychosocial resilience training: a pilot study of the *READY* program." *Psychology, health & medicine* 15, no. 3 (2010): 266–277.

Cohn, Michael A., Barbara L. Fredrickson, Stephanie L. Brown, Joseph A. Mikels, and Anne M. Conway. "Happiness unpacked: positive emotions increase life satisfaction by building resilience." *Emotion* 9, no. 3 (2009): 361–368.

Fletcher, David, and Mustafa Sarkar. "Psychological resilience: A review and critique of definitions, concepts, and theory." *European psychologist* 18 (2013): 12–23.

Loprinzi, Caitlin E., Kavita Prasad, Darrell R. Schroeder, and Amit Sood. "Stress Management and Resilience Training (SMART) program to decrease stress and enhance resilience among breast cancer survivors: a pilot randomized clinical trial." *Clinical breast cancer* 11, no. 6 (2011): 364–368.

Luthar, Suniya S., Dante Cicchetti, and Bronwyn Becker. "The construct of resilience: A critical evaluation and guidelines for future work." *Child development* 71, no. 3 (2000): 543–562.

Masten, Ann S. "Ordinary magic: Resilience processes in development." *American psychologist* 56, no. 3 (2001): 227–238.

Miller, Christian B., R. Michael Furr, Angela Knobel, and William Fleeson, eds. *Character: new directions from philosophy, psychology, and theology.* Oxford University Press, 2015.

Prince-Embury, Sandra. "The resiliency scales for children and adolescents, psychological symptoms, and clinical status in adolescents." *Canadian journal of school psychology* 23, no. 1 (2008): 41–56.

Richardson, Glenn E. "The metatheory of resilience and resiliency." *Journal of clinical psychology* 58, no. 3 (2002): 307–321.

Ryff, Carol D., and Burton Singer. "Psychological well-being: Meaning, measurement, and implications for psychotherapy research." *Psychotherapy and psychosomatics* 65, no. 1 (1996): 14–23.

Seery, Mark D., E. Alison Holman, and Roxane Cohen Silver. "Whatever does not kill us: Cumulative lifetime adversity, vulnerability, and resilience." *Journal of personality and social psychology* 99, no. 6 (2010): 1025–1041.

Sood, Amit, Kavita Prasad, Darrell Schroeder, and Prathibha Varkey. "Stress management and resilience training among Department of Medicine faculty: a pilot randomized clinical trial." *Journal of general internal medicine* 26, no. 8 (2011): 858–861.

Southwick, Steven M., George A. Bonanno, Ann S. Masten, Catherine Panter-Brick, and Rachel Yehuda. "Resilience definitions, theory, and challenges: interdisciplinary perspectives." *European journal of psychotraumatology* 5, no. 1 (2014): 25338.

Urry, Heather L., Jack B. Nitschke, Isa Dolski, Daren C. Jackson, Kim M. Dalton, Corrina J. Mueller, Melissa A. Rosenkranz, Carol D. Ryff, Burton H. Singer, and Richard J. Davidson. "Making a life worth living: Neural correlates of well-being." *Psychological science* 15, no. 6 (2004): 367–372.

CENTERS AND PROGRAMS

Center for Compassion and Altruism Research and Education (ccare .stanford.edu)

Center for Mindfulness, UMass (https://www.umassmed.edu/cfm/)

Center for Mindful Self-Compassion (https://centerformsc.org/)

Collaborative for Academic, Social, and Emotional Learning (www.casel .org)

Greater Good Science Center, University of California at Berkeley (https:// greatergood.berkeley.edu)

Openground (http://www.openground.com.au/)

The Penn Resilience Program and PERMA Workshops (https://ppc.sas .upenn.edu/services/penn-resilience-training)

Positive Psychology Center, University of Pennsylvania (https://ppc.sas .upenn.edu/)

Spirit Rock Meditation Center (https://www.spiritrock.org/)

The Wellbeing and Resilience Centre, South Australian Health and Medical Research Institute (www.wellbeingandresilience.com)

The Young Foundation (https://youngfoundation.org/)

COMPASSION

Barnard, Laura K., and John F. Curry. "Self-compassion: Conceptualizations, correlates, & interventions." *Review of general psychology* 15, no. 4 (2011): 289–303.

Neff, Kristin D., Kristin L. Kirkpatrick, and Stephanie S. Rude. "Self-compassion and adaptive psychological functioning." *Journal of research in personality* 41, no. 1 (2007): 139–154.

Neff, Kristin D., Stephanie S. Rude, and Kristin L. Kirkpatrick. "An examination of self-compassion in relation to positive psychological functioning and personality traits." *Journal of research in personality* 41, no. 4 (2007): 908–916.

MINDFULNESS

Analayo. *Satipatthana: The direct path to realization.* Windhorse Publications, 2004.

Baumeister, Roy F., and Mark R. Leary. "The need to belong: desire for interpersonal attachments as a fundamental human motivation." *Psychological bulletin* 117, no. 3 (1995): 497–529.

Brown, Kirk Warren, and Richard M. Ryan. "The benefits of being present: mindfulness and its role in psychological well-being." *Journal of personality and social psychology* 84, no. 4 (2003): 822–848.

Davidson, Richard J., Jon Kabat-Zinn, Jessica Schumacher, Melissa Rosenkranz, Daniel Muller, Saki F. Santorelli, Ferris Urbanowski, Anne Harrington, Katherine Bonus, and John F. Sheridan. "Alterations in brain and immune function produced by mindfulness meditation." *Psychosomatic medicine* 65, no. 4 (2003): 564–570.

Hölzel, Britta K., Sara W. Lazar, Tim Gard, Zev Schuman-Olivier, David R. Vago, and Ulrich Ott. "How does mindfulness meditation work? Proposing mechanisms of action from a conceptual and neural perspective." *Perspectives on psychological science* 6, no. 6 (2011): 537–559.

Porges, Stephen W. "Orienting in a defensive world: Mammalian modifications of our evolutionary heritage. A polyvagal theory." *Psychophysiology* 32, no. 4 (1995): 301–318.

Shapiro, Shauna L., Linda E. Carlson, John A. Astin, and Benedict Freedman. "Mechanisms of mindfulness." *Journal of clinical psychology* 62, no. 3 (2006): 373–386.

Tang, Yi-Yuan, Yinghua Ma, Junhong Wang, Yaxin Fan, Shigang Feng, Qilin Lu, Qingbao Yu, et al. "Short-term meditation training improves attention and self-regulation." *Proceedings of the national academy of sciences* 104, no. 43 (2007): 17152–17156.

LEARNING

Baumeister, Roy F., Ellen Bratslavsky, Catrin Finkenauer, and Kathleen D. Vohs. "Bad is stronger than good." *Review of general psychology* 5, no. 4 (2001): 323–370.

Crick, Francis, and Christof Koch. "A framework for consciousness." *Nature neuroscience* 6, no. 2 (2003): 119–126.

Kandel, Eric R. *In search of memory: The emergence of a new science of mind.* W. W. Norton & Company, 2007.

Lyubomirsky, Sonja, Kennon M. Sheldon, and David Schkade. "Pursuing happiness: The architecture of sustainable change." *Review of general psychology* 9, no. 2 (2005): 111–131.

Nader, Karim. "Memory traces unbound." *Trends in neurosciences* 26, no. 2 (2003): 65–72.

Rozin, Paul, and Edward B. Royzman. "Negativity bias, negativity dominance, and contagion." *Personality and social psychology review* 5, no. 4 (2001): 296–320.

Wilson, Margaret. "Six views of embodied cognition." *Psychonomic bulletin & review* 9, no. 4 (2002): 625–636.

GRIT

Duckworth, Angela. *Grit: The power of passion and perseverance*. Simon and Schuster, 2016.

Duckworth, Angela, and James J. Gross. "Self-control and grit: Related but separable determinants of success." *Current directions in psychological science* 23, no. 5 (2014): 319–325.

Duckworth, Angela L., Christopher Peterson, Michael D. Matthews, and Dennis R. Kelly. "Grit: perseverance and passion for long-term goals." *Journal of personality and social psychology* 92, no. 6 (2007): 1087–1101.

Ratey, John J., and Eric Hagerman. *Spark: The revolutionary new science of exercise and the brain*. Little, Brown and Company, 2008.

Singh, Kamlesh, and Shalini Duggal Jha. "Positive and negative affect, and grit as predictors of happiness and life satisfaction." *Journal of the Indian academy of applied psychology* 34, no. 2 (2008): 40–45.

GRATITUDE

Emmons, Robert A. *Thanks! How the new science of gratitude can make you happier*. Houghton Mifflin, 2007.

Fredrickson, Barbara L. "Gratitude, like other positive emotions, broadens and builds." In *The psychology of gratitude* (2004): 145–166.

Fredrickson, Barbara L. "The broaden-and-build theory of positive emotions." *Philosophical transactions of the Royal Society B: biological sciences* 359, no. 1449 (2004): 1367–1378.

Lyubomirsky, Sonja, Laura King, and Ed Diener. "The benefits of frequent positive affect: does happiness lead to success?" *Psychological bulletin*, 131, no. 6 (2005): 803–855.

Rubin, Gretchen Craft, and Gretchen Rubin. *The happiness project*. HarperCollins, 2009.

Shiota, Michelle N., Belinda Campos, Christopher Oveis, Matthew J. Hertenstein, Emiliana Simon-Thomas, and Dacher Keltner. "Beyond happiness: Building a science of discrete positive emotions." *American psychologist*, 72, no. 7 (2017): 617–643.

CONFIDENCE

Baumeister, Roy F., Jennifer D. Campbell, Joachim I. Krueger, and Kathleen D. Vohs. "Does high self-esteem cause better performance, interpersonal success, happiness, or healthier lifestyles?" *Psychological science in the public interest* 4, no. 1 (2003): 1–44.

Brown, Brené. "Shame resilience theory: A grounded theory study on women and shame." *Families in society: The journal of contemporary social services* 87, no. 1 (2006): 43–52.

Brown, Jonathon D., Keith A. Dutton, and Kathleen E. Cook. "From the top down: Self-esteem and self-evaluation." *Cognition and emotion* 15, no. 5 (2001): 615–631.

Gilbert, Paul. *The compassionate mind: A new approach to life's challenges.* New Harbinger Publications, 2010.

Longe, Olivia, Frances A. Maratos, Paul Gilbert, Gaynor Evans, Faye Volker, Helen Rockliff, and Gina Rippon. "Having a word with yourself: Neural correlates of self-criticism and self-reassurance." *NeuroImage* 49, no. 2 (2010): 1849–1856.

Robins, Richard W., and Kali H. Trzesniewski. "Self-esteem development across the lifespan." *Current directions in psychological science* 14, no. 3 (2005): 158–162.

CALM

Astin, Alexander W., and James P. Keen. "Equanimity and spirituality." *Religion & education* 33, no. 2 (2006): 39–46.

Benson, Herbert, and Miriam Z. Klipper. *The relaxation response.* HarperCollins, 1992.

Desbordes, Gaëlle, Tim Gard, Elizabeth A. Hoge, Britta K. Hölzel, Catherine Kerr, Sara W. Lazar, Andrew Olendzki, and David R. Vago. "Moving beyond mindfulness: defining equanimity as an outcome measure in meditation and contemplative research." *Mindfulness* 6, no. 2 (2015): 356–372.

Hölzel, Britta K., James Carmody, Karleyton C. Evans, Elizabeth A. Hoge, Jeffery A. Dusek, Lucas Morgan, Roger K. Pitman, and Sara W. Lazar. "Stress reduction correlates with structural changes in the amygdala." *Social cognitive and affective neuroscience* 5, no. 1 (2009): 11–17.

Lupien, Sonia J., Francoise Maheu, Mai Tu, Alexandra Fiocco, and Tania E. Schramek. "The effects of stress and stress hormones on human cognition: Implications for the field of brain and cognition." *Brain and cognition* 65, no. 3 (2007): 209–237.

MOTIVATION

Arana, F. Sergio, John A. Parkinson, Elanor Hinton, Anthony J. Holland, Adrian M. Owen, and Angela C. Roberts. "Dissociable contributions of the human amygdala and orbitofrontal cortex to incentive motivation and goal selection." *Journal of neuroscience* 23, no. 29 (2003): 9632–9638.

Berridge, Kent C. " 'Liking' and 'wanting' food rewards: brain substrates and roles in eating disorders." *Physiology & behavior* 97, no. 5 (2009): 537–550.

Berridge, Kent C., and J. Wayne Aldridge. "Special review: Decision utility, the brain, and pursuit of hedonic goals." *Social cognition* 26, no. 5 (2008): 621–646.

Berridge, Kent C., Terry E. Robinson, and J. Wayne Aldridge. "Dissecting components of reward: 'liking', 'wanting', and learning." *Current opinion in pharmacology* 9, no. 1 (2009): 65–73.

Cunningham, William A., and Tobias Brosch. "Motivational salience: Amygdala tuning from traits, needs, values, and goals." *Current directions in psychological science* 21, no. 1 (2012): 54–59.

Duhigg, Charles. *The power of habit: Why we do what we do in life and business.* Random House, 2012.

Nix, Glen A., Richard M. Ryan, John B. Manly, and Edward L. Deci. "Revitalization through self-regulation: The effects of autonomous and controlled motivation on happiness and vitality." *Journal of experimental social psychology* 35, no. 3 (1999): 266–284.

Tindell, Amy J., Kyle S. Smith, Kent C. Berridge, and J. Wayne Aldridge. "Dynamic computation of incentive salience: 'Wanting' what was never 'liked'." *Journal of neuroscience* 29, no. 39 (2009): 12220–12228.

INTIMACY

Bowlby, John. *A secure base: Clinical applications of attachment theory.* Vol. 393. Taylor & Francis, 2005.

Bretherton, Inge. "The origins of attachment theory: John Bowlby and Mary Ainsworth." *Developmental psychology* 28, no. 5 (1992): 759–775.

Eisenberger, Naomi I., Matthew D. Lieberman, and Kipling D. Williams. "Does rejection hurt? An fMRI study of social exclusion." *Science* 302, no. 5643 (2003): 290–292.

Feeney, Judith A., and Patricia Noller. "Attachment style as a predictor of adult romantic relationships." *Journal of personality and social psychology* 58, no. 2 (1990): 281–291.

House, James S. "Social isolation kills, but how and why?" *Psychosomatic medicine* 63, no. 2 (2001): 273–274.

Panksepp, Jaak. "Oxytocin effects on emotional processes: separation distress, social bonding, and relationships to psychiatric disorders." *Annals of the New York Academy of Sciences* 652, no. 1 (1992): 243–252.

Schaffer, H. Rudolph, and Peggy E. Emerson. "The development of social attachments in infancy." *Monographs of the society for research in child development* (1964): 1–77.

COURAGE

Altucher, James, and Claudia Azula Altucher. *The power of no: Because one little word can bring health, abundance, and happiness.* Hay House, 2014.

Goud, Nelson H. "Courage: Its nature and development." *The journal of humanistic counseling* 44, no. 1 (2005): 102–116.

Ng, Sik Hung, and James J. Bradac. *Power in language: Verbal communication and social influence.* Sage Publications, Inc., 1993.

Pury, Cynthia L. S., Robin M. Kowalski, and Jana Spearman. "Distinctions between general and personal courage." *The journal of positive psychology* 2, no. 2 (2007): 99–114.

Rosenberg, Marshall B. *Nonviolent communication: A language of life* (3rd ed.). Puddledancer Press, 2015.

ASPIRATION

Brown, Brené. *Daring greatly: How the courage to be vulnerable transforms the way we live, love, parent, and lead.* Gotham, 2012.

Deci, Edward L., and Richard M. Ryan. "Self-determination theory: A macrotheory of human motivation, development, and health." *Canadian psychology/Psychologie canadienne* 49, no. 3 (2008): 182–185.

King, Laura A. "The health benefits of writing about life goals." *Personality and social psychology bulletin* 27, no. 7 (2001): 798–807.

Mahone, Charles H. "Fear of failure and unrealistic vocational aspiration." *The journal of abnormal and social psychology* 60, no. 2 (1960): 253–261.

Yousafzai, Malala. *I am Malala: The girl who stood up for education and was shot by the Taliban.* Hachette UK, 2013.

GENEROSITY

Dass, Ram, and Paul Gorman. *How can I help? Stories and reflections on service.* Knopf, 2011.

Doty, James R. *Into the magic shop: A neurosurgeon's quest to discover the mysteries of the brain and the secrets of the heart.* Avery, 2015.

Eisenberg, Nancy, and Paul A. Miller. "The relation of empathy to prosocial and related behaviors." *Psychological bulletin* 101, no. 1 (1987): 91–119.

Fredrickson, Barbara L., Michael A. Cohn, Kimberly A. Coffey, Jolynn Pek, and Sandra M. Finkel. "Open hearts build lives: positive emotions, induced through loving-kindness meditation, build consequential personal resources." *Journal of personality and social psychology* 95, no. 5 (2008): 1045–1062.

Haley, Kevin J., and Daniel M. T. Fessler. "Nobody's watching? Subtle cues affect generosity in an anonymous economic game." *Evolution and human behavior* 26, no. 3 (2005): 245–256.

Zak, Paul J., Angela A. Stanton, and Sheila Ahmadi. "Oxytocin increases generosity in humans." *PLOS one* 2, no. 11 (2007): e1128.

INDEX

ABOUT THE AUTHORS

Rick Hanson, Ph.D., is a psychologist, senior fellow of the Greater Good Science Center at UC Berkeley, and *New York Times* bestselling author. Available in twenty-six languages, his books include *Hardwiring Happiness*, *Buddha's Brain*, *Just One Thing*, and *Mother Nurture*. He edits the *Wise Brain Bulletin* and has numerous audio programs. A summa cum laude graduate of UCLA and founder of the Wellspring Institute for Neuroscience and Contemplative Wisdom, he has been an invited speaker at NASA, Oxford, Stanford, Harvard, and other major universities, and has taught in meditation centers worldwide. Dr. Hanson is a former trustee of Saybrook University, served on the board of Spirit Rock Meditation Center, and was president of the board of FamilyWorks, a community agency. He began meditating in 1974, trained in several traditions, and leads a weekly meditation gathering in San Rafael, California. He enjoys rock climbing. He and his wife have two adult children.

Forrest Hanson is a writer and a business consultant. He edits Eusophi, a website dedicated to sharing high-quality content from experts in the fields of happiness, health, wealth, and wisdom. A UC Berkeley graduate, he lives in the San Francisco Bay Area and pursues dancing as a serious hobby.